Lab Manual
Module J

HOLT McDOUGAL

 HOUGHTON MIFFLIN HARCOURT

Acknowledgements for Covers

Cover Photo Credits

Fiber-optic cable (bg) ©Dennis O'Clair/Stone/Getty Images; *pacific wheel* (l) ©Geoffrey George/Getty Images; *snowboarder* (cl) ©Jonathan Nourok/Photographer's Choice/Getty Images; *water droplet* (cr) ©L. Clarke/Corbis; *molecular structure* (r) ©Stockbyte/Getty Images

ISBN 978-0-547-59321-0

  3 4 5 6 7 8 9 10   0982   20 19 18 17 16 15 14 13 12
4500364970   A B C D E F G

Contents

INTRODUCTION

Using Your *ScienceFusion* Lab Program v
Science Kit vi
Online Lab Resources vii

TEACHER LAB SAFETY

Making Your Laboratory a Safe Place ix
Safety with Chemicals x
Safety with Animals xi
Safety with Microbes xii
Personal Protective Equipment xiii

STUDENT LAB SAFETY

Safety Symbols xiv
Safety in the Laboratory xvi
Safety in the Field xviii
Laboratory Techniques xix
Student Safety Quiz xxiii
Student Safety Contract xxvii

Unit 1 Introduction to Waves

Lesson 1 Quick Lab 1: Investigate Waves 1
Lesson 1 Quick Lab 2: Water Waves 5
Lesson 2 Quick Lab 1: Investigate Frequency 9
Lesson 2 Quick Lab 2: Waves on a Spring 13
Lesson 2 Exploration Lab 1: Investigate Wavelength 17

Unit 2 Sound

Lesson 1 Quick Lab 1: Investigate Sound Energy 27
Lesson 1 Quick Lab 2: Different Instrument Sounds 31
Lesson 1 Quick Lab 3: Investigate Loudness 36
Lesson 1 Exploration Lab 1: Sound Idea 40
Lesson 2 Quick Lab 1: Resonance in a Bottle 50
Lesson 2 Quick Lab 2: The Speed of Sound 53
Lesson 2 STEM Lab 1: Echoes 58
Lesson 3 Quick Lab 1: Making an AM Radio Transmitter 71
Lesson 3 Quick Lab 2: Sound Recording and Playback 75

Unit 3 Light

Lesson 1 Quick Lab 1: Investigate the Electromagnetic Spectrum 79

Lesson 1 Quick Lab 2: White Light 83

Lesson 2 Quick Lab 1: Why Is the Sky Blue? 87

Lesson 2 Quick Lab 2: Refraction with Water 91

Lesson 2 Exploration Lab 1: Comparing Colors of Objects
in Different Colors of Light 95

Lesson 3 Quick Lab 1: Spoon Images 105

Lesson 3 Quick Lab 2: Mirror Images 109

Lesson 3 STEM Lab 1: Light Maze 112

Lesson 4 Quick Lab 1: Shapes and Sight 121

Lesson 4 Quick Lab 2: Investigating Vision 125

Lesson 5 Quick Lab 1: Light Technology in Color Monitors 129

Lesson 5 Quick Lab 2: Total Internal Reflection 132

Lesson 5 Exploration Lab 1: Investigating Artificial Light 136

Using Your *ScienceFusion* Lab Program

Your *ScienceFusion* Lab Program is designed to include activities that address a variety of student levels, inquiry levels, time availability, and materials. In this Lab Manual, you will find that each student activity is preceded by Teacher Resources with valuable information about the activity.

Activity Type: Quick Lab

Each lesson within each unit is supported by two to three short activities called Quick Labs. Quick Labs involve simple materials and set-up. The student portion of each Quick Lab should take less than 30 minutes. Each Quick Lab includes Teacher Resources and one Student Datasheet.

Activity Types: Exploration Lab, Field Lab, and S.T.E.M. Lab

Each unit is supported by one to four additional labs that require one or more class periods to complete. Each Exploration, Field, and S.T.E.M. Lab includes Teacher Resources and two Student Datasheets. Each Student Datasheet is targeted to address different inquiry levels. Below is a description of each lab:

- **Exploration Labs** are traditional lab activities. The labs are designed to be conducted with standard laboratory equipment and materials.
- **Field Labs** are lab activities that are partially or completely performed outside the classroom or laboratory.
- **S.T.E.M. Labs** are lab activities that focus on Science, Technology, Engineering, and Math skills.

Inquiry Level

The inquiry level of each activity indicates the level at which students direct the activity. An activity that is entirely student-directed is often called Open Inquiry or Independent Inquiry. True Open or Independent Inquiry is based on a question posed by students, uses experimental processes designed by students, and requires students to find the connections between data and content. These types of activities result from student interest in the world around them. The *ScienceFusion* Lab Program provides activities that allow for a wide variety of student involvement.

- DIRECTED **Inquiry** is the least student-directed of the inquiry levels. Directed Inquiry activities provide students with an introduction to content, a procedure to follow, and direction on how to organize and analyze data.

- GUIDED **Inquiry** indicates that an activity is moderately student-directed. Guided Inquiry activities require students to select materials, procedural steps, data analysis techniques, or other aspects of the activity.

- INDEPENDENT **Inquiry** indicates that an activity is highly student-directed. Though students are provided with ideas, partial procedures, or suggestions, they are responsible for selecting many aspects of the activity.

Each Quick Lab includes one Student Datasheet that is written to support the inquiry level indicated on the Teacher Resources. Each Exploration Lab, Field Lab, and S.T.E.M. Lab includes two Student Datasheets, each written to support an inquiry level. In addition, the Teacher Resources includes one or more modification suggestions to adjust the inquiry level.

Student Level

The *ScienceFusion* Lab Program is designed to provide successful experiences for all levels of students.

- BASIC activities focus on introductory content and concepts taught in the lesson. These activities can be used with any level of student, including those who may have learning or language difficulties, but they may not provide a challenge for advanced students.

- GENERAL activities are appropriate for most students.

- ADVANCED activities require good understanding of the content and concepts in the lesson or ask students to manipulate content to arrive at the learning objective. Advanced activities may provide a challenge to advanced students, but they may be difficult for average or basic-level students.

Lab Ratings

Each activity is rated on three criteria to provide you with information that you may find useful when determining if an activity is appropriate for your resources.

- **Teacher Prep** rating indicates the amount of preparation you will need to provide before students can perform the activity.

- **Student Setup** rating indicates the amount of preparation students will need to perform before they begin to collect data.

- **Cleanup** rating indicates the amount of effort required to dispose of materials and disassemble the set-up of the activity.

Teacher Notes

Information and background that may be helpful to you can be found in the Teacher Notes section of the Teacher Resources. The information includes hints and a list of skills that students will practice during the activity.

Science Kit

Hands-on materials needed to complete all the labs in the Lab Manual for each module have been conveniently configured into consumable and non-consumable kits. Common materials provided by parents or your school/district are not included in the kits. Laboratory equipment commonly found in most schools has been separately packaged in a Grades 6–8 Inquiry Equipment Kit. This economical option allows schools to buy equipment only if they need it and can be shared among teachers and across grade levels. For more information on the material kits or to order, contact your local Holt McDougal sales representative or call customer service at 800-462-6595.

Online Lab Resources

The *ScienceFusion* Lab Program offers many additional resources online through our web site thinkcentral.com. These resources include:

Teacher Notes, Transparencies, and **Copymasters** are found in the Online Toolkit. Student-friendly tutorial Transparencies are available to print as transparencies or handouts. Each set of Transparencies is supported by Teacher Notes that include background information, teaching tips, and techniques. Teacher Notes, Transparencies, and Copymatsters are available to teach a broad range of skills.

- **Modeling Experimental Design** Teacher Notes and Transparencies cover Scientific Methods skills, such as Making Qualitative Observations, Developing a Hypothesis, and Making Valid Inferences.

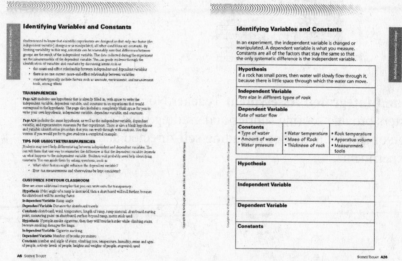

- **Writing in the Sciences** Teacher Notes and Transparencies teach written communication skills, such as Writing a Lab Report and Maintaining a Science Notebook. In addition, the Lab Report Template provides a structured format that students can use as the basis for their own lab reports.

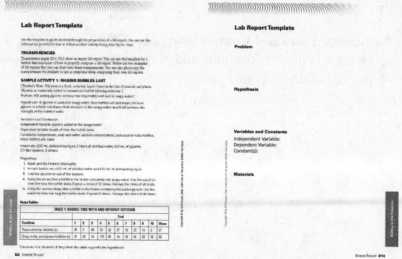

- **Math in Science Tools** Teacher Notes and Transparencies teach the math skills that are needed for data analysis in labs. These Teacher Notes and Transparencies support the S.T.E.M. concepts found throughout the *ScienceFusion* program.

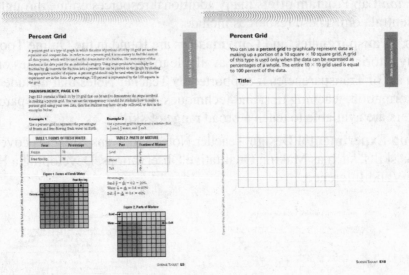

- **Rubrics and Integrated Assessment** Teacher Notes and Copymasters provide scoring rubrics and grading support for a range of student activities including self-directed and guided experiments.

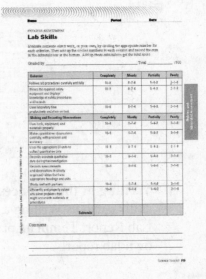

- **Planning for Science Fairs and Competitions** Teacher Notes and Copymasters provide planning and preparation techniques for science fairs and other competitions.

Making Your Laboratory a Safe Place

Concern for safety must begin before any activity in the classroom and before students enter the lab. A careful review of the facilities should be a basic part of preparation for each school term. You should investigate the physical environment, identify any safety risks, and inspect your work areas for compliance with safety regulations.

The review of the lab should be thorough, and all safety issues must be addressed immediately. Keep a file of your review, and add to the list each year. This will allow you to continue to raise the standard of safety in your lab and classroom.

Many classroom experiments, demonstrations, and other activities are classics that have been used for years. This familiarity may lead to a comfort that can obscure inherent safety concerns. Review all experiments, demonstrations, and activities for safety concerns before presenting them to the class. Identify and eliminate potential safety hazards.

1. **Identify the Risks** Before introducing any activity, demonstration, or experiment to the class, analyze it and consider what could possibly go wrong. Carefully review the list of materials to make sure they are safe. Inspect the equipment in your lab or classroom to make sure it is in good working order. Read the procedures to make sure they are safe. Record any hazards or concerns you identify.

2. **Evaluate the Risks** Minimize the risks you identified in the last step without sacrificing learning. Remember that no activity you perform in the lab or classroom is worth risking injury. Thus, extremely hazardous activities, or those that violate your school's policies, must be eliminated. For activities that present smaller risks, analyze each risk carefully to determine its likelihood. If the pedagogical value of the activity does not outweigh the risks, the activity must be eliminated.

3. **Select Controls to Address Risks** Even low-risk activities require controls to eliminate or minimize the risks. Make sure that in devising controls you do not substitute an equally or more hazardous alternative. Some control methods include the following:

   • Explicit verbal and written warnings may be added or posted.

   • Equipment may be rebuilt or relocated, parts may be replaced, or equipment be replaced entirely by safer alternatives.

   • Risky procedures may be eliminated.

   • Activities may be changed from student activities to teacher demonstrations.

4. **Implement and Review Selected Controls** Controls do not help if they are forgotten or not enforced. The implementation and review of controls should be as systematic and thorough as the initial analysis of safety concerns in the lab and laboratory activities.

Safety with Chemicals

Label student reagent containers with the substance's name and hazard class(es) (flammable, reactive, etc.). Dispose of hazardous waste chemicals according to federal, state, and local regulations. Refer to the MSDS for recommended disposal procedures. Remove all sources of flames, sparks, and heat from the laboratory when any flammable material is being used.

Material Safety Data Sheets

The purpose of a Material Safety Data Sheet (MSDS) is to provide readily accessible information on chemical substances commonly used in the science laboratory or in industry. The MSDS should be kept on file and referred to BEFORE handling ANY chemical. The MSDS can also be used to instruct students on chemical hazards, to evaluate spill and disposal procedures, and to warn of incompatibility with other chemicals or mixtures.

Storing Chemicals

Never store chemicals alphabetically, as this greatly increases the risk of promoting a violent reaction.

Storage Suggestions

1. Always lock the storeroom and all its cabinets when not in use.
2. Students should not be allowed in the storeroom and preparation area.
3. Avoid storing chemicals on the floor of the storeroom.
4. Do not store chemicals above eye level or on the top shelf in the storeroom.
5. Be sure shelf assemblies are firmly secured to the walls.
6. Provide anti-roll lips on all shelves.
7. Shelving should be constructed out of wood. Metal cabinets and shelves are easily corroded.
8. Avoid metal, adjustable shelf supports and clips. They can corrode, causing shelves to collapse.
9. Acids, flammables, poisons, and oxidizers should each be stored in their own locking storage cabinet.

Safety with Animals

It is recommended that teachers follow the NABT Position Statement
"The Use of Animals in Biology Education" issued by the National Association of
Biology Teachers (available at www.nabt.org).

Safety In Handling Preserved Materials

The following practices are recommended when handling preserved specimens:

1. NEVER dissect road-kills or nonpreserved slaughterhouse materials.

2. Wear protective gloves and splash-proof safety goggles at all times when handling preserving fluids and preserved specimens and during dissection.

3. Wear lab aprons. Use of an old shirt or smock under the lab apron is recommended.

4. Conduct dissection activities in a well-ventilated area.

5. Do not allow preservation or body-cavity fluids to contact skin. Fixatives do not distinguish between living or dead tissues. Biological supply firms may use formalin-based fixatives of varying concentrations to initially fix zoological and botanical specimens. Some provide specimens that are freezedried and rehydrated in a 10% isopropyl alcohol solution. Many suppliers provide fixed botanical materials in 50% glycerin.

Reduction Of Free Formaldehyde

Currently, federal regulations mandate a permissible exposure level of 0.75 ppm for formaldehyde. Contact your supplier for Material Data Safety Sheet (MSDS) that details the amount of formaldehyde present as well as gas-emitting characteristics for individual specimens. Prewash specimens (in a loosely covered container) in running tap water for 1–4 hours to dilute the fixative. Formaldehyde may also be chemically bound (thereby reducing danger) by immersing washed specimens in a 0.5–1.0% potassium bisulfate solution overnight or by placing them in 1% phenoxyethanol holding solutions.

Safety with Microbes

WHAT YOU CAN'T SEE CAN HURT YOU

Pathogenic (disease-causing) microorganisms are not appropriate investigation tools in the high school laboratory and should never be used.

Consult with the school nurse to screen students whose immune systems may be compromised by illness or who may be receiving immunosuppressive drug therapy. Such individuals are extraordinarily sensitive to potential infection from generally harmless microorganisms and should not participate in laboratory activities unless permitted to do so by a physician. Do not allow students who have any open cuts, abrasions, or open sores to work with microorganisms.

HOW TO USE ASEPTIC TECHNIQUE

- Demonstrate correct aseptic technique to students prior to conducting a lab activity. Never pipet liquid media by mouth. When possible, use sterile cotton applicator sticks instead of inoculating loops and Bunsen burner flames for culture inoculation. Remember to use appropriate precautions when disposing of cotton applicator sticks: they should be autoclaved or sterilized before disposal.
- Treat all microbes as pathogenic. Seal with tape all petri dishes containing bacterial cultures. Do not use blood agar plates, and never attempt to cultivate microbes from a human or animal source.
- Never dispose of microbe cultures without sterilizing them first. Autoclave or steam-sterilize at 120°C and 15 psi for 15 to 20 minutes all used cultures and any materials that have come in contact with them. If these devices are not available, flood or immerse these articles in full-strength household bleach for 30 minutes, and then discard. Use the autoclave or steam sterilizer yourself; do not allow students to use these devices.
- Wash all lab surfaces with a disinfectant solution before and after handling bacterial cultures.

HOW TO HANDLE BACTERIOLOGICAL SPILLS

- Never allow students to clean up bacteriological spills. Keep on hand a spill kit containing 500 mL of full-strength household bleach, biohazard bags (autoclavable), forceps, and paper towels.
- In the event of a bacterial spill, cover the area with a layer of paper towels. Wet the paper towels with bleach, and allow them to stand for 15 to 20 minutes. Wearing gloves and using forceps, place the residue in the biohazard bag. If broken glass is present, use a brush and dustpan to collect material, and place it in a suitably marked puncture-resistant container for disposal.

Personal Protective Equipment

Chemical goggles (Meeting ANSI Standard Z87.1) These should be worn with any chemical or chemical solution other than water, when heating substances, using any mechanical device, or observing physical processes that could eject an object.

Face shield (Meeting ANSI Standard Z87.1) Use in combination with eye goggles when working with corrosives.

Contact lenses The wearing of contact lenses for cosmetic reasons should be prohibited in the laboratory. If a student must wear contact lenses prescribed by a physician, that student should be instructed to wear eye-cup safety goggles, similar to swimmer's cup goggles, meeting ANSI Standard Z87.1.

Eye-wash station The device must be capable of delivering a copious, gentle flow of water to both eyes for at least 15 minutes. Portable liquid supply devices are not satisfactory and should not be used. A plumbed-in fixture or a perforated spray head on the end of a hose attached to a plumbed-in outlet is suitable if it is designed for use as an eye-wash fountain and meets ANSI Standard Z358.1. It must be within a 30-second walking distance from any spot in the room.

Safety shower (Meeting ANSI Standard Z358.1) Location should be within a 30-second walking distance from any spot in the room. Students should be instructed in the use of the safety shower in the event of a fire or chemical splash on their body that cannot simply be washed off.

Gloves Polyethylene, neoprene rubber, or disposable plastic may be used. Nitrile or butyl rubber gloves are recommended when handling corrosives.

Apron Rubber-coated cloth or vinyl (nylon-coated) halter is recommended.

Student Safety in the Laboratory

Systematic, careful lab work is an essential part of any science program. The equipment and apparatus students will use present various safety hazards. You must be aware of these hazards before students engage in any lab activity. The Teacher Resource Pages at the beginning of each lab in this Lab Manual will guide you in properly directing the equipment use during the experiments. Photocopy the information on the following pages for students. These safety rules always apply in the lab and in the field.

Safety Symbols

The following safety symbols will appear in the instructions for labs and activities to emphasize important notes of caution. Learn what they represent so that you can take the appropriate precautions.

	### Eye Protection • Wear approved safety goggles at all times in the lab as directed. • If chemicals get into your eyes, flush your eyes immediately. • Do not wear contact lenses in the lab. • Do not look directly at the sun or any intense light source or laser.
	### Hand Safety • Do not cut an object while holding the object in your hand. • Wear appropriate protective gloves when working with an open flame, chemicals, solutions, or wild or unknown plants. • Use a heat-resistant mitt to handle equipment that may be hot.
	### Clothing Protection • Wear an apron or lab coat at all times in the lab. • Tie back long hair, secure loose clothing, and remove loose jewelry so that they do not knock over equipment, get caught in moving parts, or come into contact with hazardous materials or electrical connections. • Do not wear open-toed shoes, sandals, or canvas shoes in the lab. • When outside for lab, wear long sleeves, long pants, socks, and closed shoes.
	### Glassware Safety • Inspect glassware before use; do not use chipped or cracked glassware. • Use heat-resistant glassware for heating materials or storing hot liquids. • Notify your teacher immediately if a piece of glassware or a light bulb breaks.
	### Sharp-Object Safety • Use extreme care when handling all sharp and pointed instruments. • Cut objects on a suitable surface, always in a direction away from your body. • Be aware of sharp objects or edges on equipment or apparatus.
	### Chemical Safety • If a chemical gets on your skin, on your clothing, or in your eyes, rinse it immediately (shower, faucet or eyewash fountain) and alert your teacher. • Do not clean up spilled chemicals yourself unless your teacher directs you to do so. • Do not inhale any gas or vapor unless your teacher directs you to do so. • Handle materials that emit vapors or gases in a well-ventilated area.

Electrical Safety

- Do not use equipment with frayed electrical cords or loose plugs.
- Fasten electrical cords to work surfaces by using tape.
- Do not use electrical equipment near water or when clothing or hands are wet.
- Hold the plug housing when you plug in or unplug equipment.
- Be aware that wire coils in electrical circuits may heat up rapidly.

Heating Safety

- Be aware of any source of flames, sparks, or heat (such as open flames, heating coils, or hot plates) before working with any flammable substances.
- Avoid using open flames.
- Know the location of lab fire extinguishers and fire-safety blankets.
- Know your school's fire-evacuation routes.
- If your clothing catches on fire, walk to the lab shower to put out the fire.
- Never leave a hot plate unattended while it is turned on or while it is cooling.
- Use tongs or appropriate insulated holders when handling heated objects.
- Allow all equipment to cool before storing it.

Plant Safety

- Do not eat any part of a plant or plant seed.
- When outside, do not pick any wild plants unless your teacher instructs you to do so.
- Wash your hands thoroughly after handling any part of a plant.

Animal Safety

- Handle animals only as your teacher directs.
- Treat animals carefully and respectfully.
- Wash your hands thoroughly after handling any animal.

Proper Waste Disposal

- Clean and sanitize all work surfaces and personal protective equipment after each lab period as directed by your teacher.
- Dispose of hazardous materials only as directed by your teacher.
- Dispose of sharp objects (such as broken glass) in the appropriate sharps or broken glass container as directed by your teacher.

Hygienic Care

- Keep your hands away from your face while you are working on any activity.
- Wash your hands thoroughly before you leave the lab or after any activity.
- Remove contaminated clothing immediately.

Safety in the Laboratory

1. **Always wear a lab apron and safety goggles.** Wear these safety devices whenever you are in the lab, not just when you are working on an experiment.

2. **No contact lenses in the lab.** Contact lenses should not be worn during any investigations in which you are using chemicals (even if you are wearing goggles). In the event of an accident, chemicals can get behind contact lenses and cause serious damage before the lenses can be removed. If your doctor requires that you wear contact lenses instead of glasses, you should wear eye-cup safety goggles in the lab. Ask your doctor or your teacher how to use this very important and special eye protection.

3. **Personal apparel should be appropriate for laboratory work.** On lab days, avoid wearing long necklaces, dangling bracelets, bulky jewelry, and bulky or loose-fitting clothing. Long hair should be tied back. Loose, flopping, or dangling items may get caught in moving parts, accidentally contact electrical connections, or interfere with the investigation in some potentially hazardous manner. In addition, chemical fumes may react with some jewelry, such as pearls, and ruin them. Cotton clothing is preferable to wool, nylon, or polyesters. Wear shoes that will protect your feet from chemical spills and falling objects— no open-toed shoes or sandals and no shoes with woven leather straps.

4. **NEVER work alone in the laboratory.** Work in the lab only while supervised by your teacher. Do not leave equipment unattended while it is in operation.

5. **Only books and notebooks needed for the activity should be in the lab.** Only the lab notebook and perhaps the textbook should be used. Keep other books, backpacks, purses, and similar items in your desk, locker, or designated storage area.

6. **Read the entire activity before entering the lab.** Your teacher will review any applicable safety precautions before you begin the lab activity. If you are not sure of something, ask your teacher about it.

7. Always heed safety symbols and cautions in the instructions for the experiments, in handouts, and on posters in the room, and always heed cautions given verbally by your teacher. They are provided for your safety.

8. Know the proper fire drill procedures and the locations of fire exits and emergency equipment. Make sure you know the procedures to follow in case of a fire or other emergency.

9. **If your clothing catches on fire, do not run;** WALK to the safety shower, stand under the showerhead, and turn the water on. Call to your teacher while you do this.

10. **Report all accidents to the teacher** IMMEDIATELY, no matter how minor. In addition, if you get a headache or feel ill or dizzy, tell your teacher immediately.

Safety in the Laboratory continued

11. **Report all spills to your teacher immediately.** Call your teacher, rather than cleaning a spill yourself. Your teacher will tell you if it is safe for you to clean up the spill. If it is not safe for you to clean up the spill, your teacher will know how the spill should be cleaned up safely.

12. If a lab directs you to design your own experiments, procedures must be approved by your teacher BEFORE you begin work.

13. DO NOT perform unauthorized experiments or use equipment or apparatus in a manner for which they were not intended. Use only materials and equipment listed in the activity equipment list or authorized by your teacher. Steps in a procedure should only be performed as described in the lab manual or as approved by your teacher.

14. **Stay alert while in the lab, and proceed with caution.** Be aware of others near you or your equipment when you are proceeding with the experiment. If you are not sure of how to proceed, ask your teacher for help.

15. **Horseplay in the lab is very dangerous.** Laboratory equipment and apparatus are not toys; never play in the lab or use lab time or equipment for anything other than their intended purpose.

16. Food, beverages, and chewing gum are NEVER permitted in the laboratory.

17. **NEVER taste chemicals.** Do not touch chemicals or allow them to contact areas of bare skin.

18. **Use extreme CAUTION when working with hot plates or other heating devices.** Keep your head, hands, hair, and clothing away from the flame or heating area, and turn the devices off when they are not in use. Remember that metal surfaces connected to the heated area will become hot by conduction. Gas burners should be lit only with a spark lighter. Make sure all heating devices and gas valves are turned off before leaving the laboratory. Never leave a hot plate or other heating device unattended when it is in use. Remember that many metal, ceramic, and glass items do not always look hot when they are heated. Allow all items to cool before storing them.

19. **Exercise caution when working with electrical equipment.** Do not use electrical equipment that has frayed or twisted wires. Be sure your hands are dry before you use electrical equipment. Do not let electrical cords dangle from work stations; dangling cords can cause tripping or electrical shocks.

20. **Keep work areas and apparatus clean and neat.** Always clean up any clutter made during the course of lab work, rearrange apparatus in an orderly manner, and report any damaged or missing items.

21. Always thoroughly wash your hands with soap and water at the conclusion of each investigation.

Safety in the Field

Activities conducted outdoors require some advance planning to ensure a safe environment. The following general guidelines should be followed for fieldwork.

1. **Know your mission.** Your teacher will tell you the goal of the field trip in advance. Be sure to have your permission slip approved before the trip, and check to be sure that you have all necessary supplies for the day's activity.

2. **Find out about on-site hazards before setting out.** Determine whether poisonous plants or dangerous animals are likely to be present where you are going. Know how to identify these hazards. Find out about other hazards, such as steep or slippery terrain.

3. **Wear protective clothing.** Dress in a manner that will keep you warm, comfortable, and dry. Decide in advance whether you will need sunglasses, a hat, gloves, boots, or rain gear to suit the terrain and local weather conditions.

4. **Do not approach or touch wild animals.** If you see a threatening animal, call your teacher immediately. Avoid any living thing that may sting, bite, scratch, or otherwise cause injury.

5. **Do not touch wild plants or pick wildflowers unless specifically instructed to do so** by your teacher. Many wild plants can be irritating or toxic. Never taste any wild plant.

6. **Do not wander away from others.** Travel with a partner at all times. Stay within an area where you can be seen or heard in case you run into trouble.

7. **Report all hazards or accidents to your teacher immediately.** Even if the incident seems unimportant, let your teacher know what happened.

8. **Maintain the safety of the environment.** Do not remove anything from the field site without your teacher's permission. Stay on trails, when possible, to avoid trampling delicate vegetation. Never leave garbage behind at a field site. Leave natural areas as you found them.

Laboratory Techniques

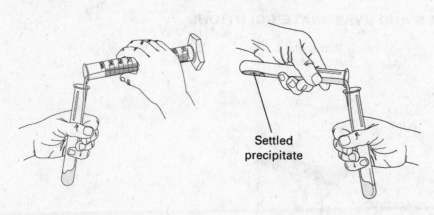

Settled
precipitate

Figure A   **Figure B**   **Figure C**

HOW TO DECANT AND TRANSFER LIQUIDS

1. The safest way to transfer a liquid from a graduated cylinder to a test tube is shown in **Figure A**. The liquid is transferred at arm's length, with the elbows slightly bent. This position enables you to see what you are doing while maintaining steady control of the equipment.

2. Sometimes, liquids contain particles of insoluble solids that sink to the bottom of a test tube or beaker. Use one of the methods shown above to separate a supernatant (the clear fluid) from insoluble solids.

    a. **Figure B** shows the proper method of decanting a supernatant liquid from a test tube.

    b. **Figure C** shows the proper method of decanting a supernatant liquid from a beaker by using a stirring rod. The rod should touch the wall of the receiving container. Hold the stirring rod against the lip of the beaker containing the supernatant. As you pour, the liquid will run down the rod and fall into the beaker resting below. When you use this method, the liquid will not run down the side of the beaker from which you are pouring.

Laboratory Techniques continued

HOW TO HEAT SUBSTANCES AND EVAPORATE SOLUTIONS

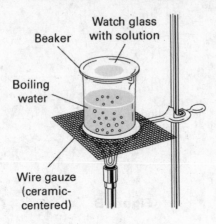

FIGURE D

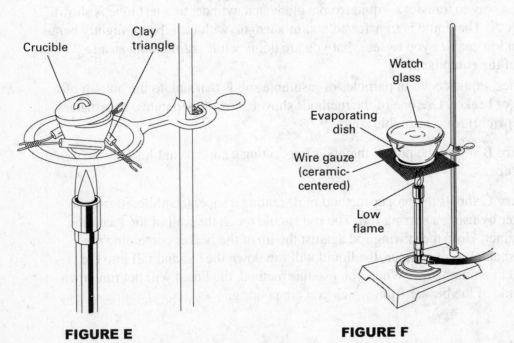

FIGURE E   **FIGURE F**

1. Use care in selecting glassware for high-temperature heating. The glassware should be heat resistant.

2. When heating glassware by using a gas flame, use a ceramic-centered wire gauze to protect glassware from direct contact with the flame. Wire gauzes can withstand extremely high temperatures and will help prevent glassware from breaking. **Figure D** shows the proper setup for evaporating a solution over a water bath.

3. In some experiments, you are required to heat a substance to high temperatures in a porcelain crucible. Figure E shows the proper apparatus setup used to accomplish this task.

4. **Figure F** shows the proper setup for evaporating a solution in a porcelain evaporating dish with a watch glass cover that prevents spattering.

Laboratory Techniques continued

5. Glassware, porcelain, and iron rings that have been heated may look cool after they are removed from a heat source, but these items can still burn your skin even after several minutes of cooling. Use tongs, test-tube holders, or heat-resistant mitts and pads whenever you handle these pieces of apparatus.

6. You can test the temperature of beakers, ring stands, wire gauzes, or other pieces of apparatus that have been heated by holding the back of your hand close to their surfaces before grasping them. You will be able to feel any energy as heat generated from the hot surfaces. DO NOT TOUCH THE APPARATUS. Allow plenty of time for the apparatus to cool before handling.

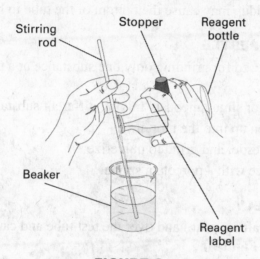

FIGURE G

HOW TO POUR LIQUID FROM A REAGENT BOTTLE

1. Read the label at least three times before using the contents of a reagent bottle.

2. Never lay the stopper of a reagent bottle on the lab table.

3. When pouring a caustic or corrosive liquid into a beaker, use a stirring rod to avoid drips and spills. Hold the stirring rod against the lip of the reagent bottle. Estimate the amount of liquid you need, and pour this amount along the rod, into the beaker. See **Figure G**.

4. Extra precaution should be taken when handling a bottle of acid. Remember the following important rules: Never add water to any concentrated acid, particularly sulfuric acid, because the mixture can splash and will generate a lot of energy as heat. To dilute any acid, add the acid to water in small quantities while stirring slowly. Remember the "triple A's"—*Always Add Acid* to water.

5. Examine the outside of the reagent bottle for any liquid that has dripped down the bottle or spilled on the counter top. Your teacher will show you the proper procedures for cleaning up a chemical spill.

6. Never pour reagents back into stock bottles. At the end of the experiment, your teacher will tell you how to dispose of any excess chemicals.

Laboratory Techniques continued

HOW TO HEAT MATERIAL IN A TEST TUBE

1. Check to see that the test tube is heat resistant.
2. Always use a test tube holder or clamp when heating a test tube.
3. Never point a heated test tube at anyone, because the liquid may splash out of the test tube.
4. Never look down into the test tube while heating it.
5. Heat the test tube from the upper portions of the tube downward, and continuously move the test tube, as shown in **Figure H**. Do not heat any one spot on the test tube. Otherwise, a pressure buildup may cause the bottom of the tube to blow out.

HOW TO USE A MORTAR AND PESTLE

1. A mortar and pestle should be used for grinding only one substance at a time. See **Figure I**.
2. Never use a mortar and pestle for simultaneously mixing different substances.
3. Place the substance to be broken up into the mortar.
4. Pound the substance with the pestle, and grind to pulverize.
5. Remove the powdered substance with a porcelain spoon.

HOW TO DETECT ODORS SAFELY

1. Test for the odor of gases by wafting your hand over the test tube and cautiously sniffing the fumes as shown in **Figure J**.
2. Do not inhale any fumes directly.
3. Use a fume hood whenever poisonous or irritating fumes are present. DO NOT waft and sniff poisonous or irritating fumes.

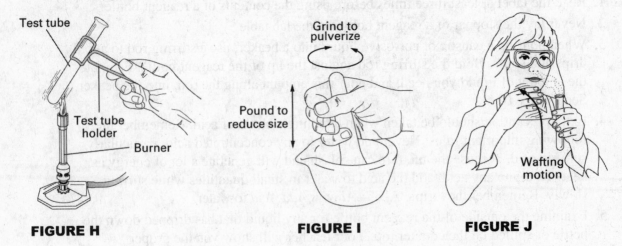

FIGURE H   **FIGURE I**   **FIGURE J**

Student Safety Quiz

Circle the letter of the BEST answer.

1. Before starting an investigation or lab procedure, you should

    a. try an experiment of your own

    b. open all containers and packages

    c. read all directions and make sure you understand them

    d. handle all the equipment to become familiar with it

2. When pouring chemicals between containers, you should hold the containers over

    a. the floor or a waste basket

    b. a fire blanket or an oven mitt

    c. an eyewash station or a water fountain

    d. a sink or your work area

3. If you get hurt or injured in any way, you should

    a. tell your teacher immediately

    b. find bandages or a first aid kit

    c. go to the principal's office

    d. get help after you finish the lab

4. If your glassware is chipped or broken, you should

    a. use it only for solid materials

    b. give it to your teacher

    c. put it back into the storage cabinet

    d. increase the damage so that it is obvious

5. If you have unused chemicals after finishing a procedure, you should

    a. pour them down a sink or drain

    b. mix them all together in a bucket

    c. put them back into their original containers

    d. throw them away where your teacher tells you to

6. If electrical equipment has a frayed cord, you should

   a. unplug the equipment by pulling on the cord

   b. let the cord hang over the side of a counter or table

   c. tell your teacher about the problem immediately

   d. wrap tape around the cord to repair it

7. If you need to determine the odor of a chemical or a solution, you should

   a. use your hand to bring fumes from the container to your nose

   b. bring the container under your nose and inhale deeply

   c. tell your teacher immediately

   d. use odor-sensing equipment

8. When working with materials that might fly into the air and hurt someone's eye, you should wear

   a. goggles

   b. an apron

   c. gloves

   d. a hat

9. Before doing experiments involving a heat source, you should know the location of the

   a. door

   b. windows

   c. fire extinguisher

   d. overhead lights

10. If you get a chemical in your eye, you should

    a. wash your hands immediately

    b. put the lid back on the chemical container

    c. wait to see if your eye becomes irritated

    d. use the eyewash right away

11. When working with a flame or heat source, you should

    a.   tie back long hair or hair that hangs in front of your eyes

    b.   heat substances or objects inside a closed container

    c.   touch an object with your bare hand to see how hot it is

    d.   throw hot objects into the trash when you are done with them

12. As you cut with a knife or other sharp instrument, you should move the instrument

    a.   toward you

    b.   away from you

    c.   vertically

    d.   horizontally

LAB SAFETY QUIZ
Answer Key

1. C	5. D	9. C
2. D	6. C	10. D
3. A	7. A	11. A
4. B	8. A	12. B

Student Safety Contract

Read carefully the Student Safety Contract below. Then, fill in your name in the first blank, date the contract, and sign it.

Student Safety Contract
I will • read the lab investigation before coming to class • wear personal protective equipment as directed to protect my eyes, face, hands, and body while conducting class activities • follow all instructions given by the teacher • conduct myself in a responsible manner at all times in a laboratory situation I, _____, have read and agree to abide by the safety regulations as set forth above and any additional printed instructions provided by my teacher or the school district. I agree to follow all other written and oral instructions given in class. Signature: _____ Date: _____

QUICK LAB INDEPENDENT Inquiry

Investigate Waves GENERAL

👥 Student pairs

🕐 15 minutes

LAB RATINGS

LESS ← → MORE

Teacher Prep —

Student Setup —

Cleanup —

MATERIALS

For each pair
• spring toy, coiled
For each student
• safety goggles

My Notes

_____

_____

_____

_____

_____

SAFETY INFORMATION

Remind students to review all safety cautions and icons before beginning this lab. Instruct student teams to stay far enough away from each other so that the spring coils do not accidentally strike other students as the waves are being generated.

TEACHER NOTES

In this activity, students will use a spring toy to investigate wave types. Each pair of students should come up with a specific question to investigate, such as, "How does the direction of a disturbance affect the movement of a wave?" Students will devise procedures to carry out their investigations. Students will also decide how to observe and record data. After students complete their procedures, they will compare the different wave types they observed during the experiment.

Tip For best results, students should observe disturbances in the spring when it is stretched out.

Skills Focus Asking Questions, Making Observations

MODIFICATION FOR DIRECTED Inquiry

Provide students with a specific question to investigate, such as "How does the direction of a disturbance affect the movement of a wave?" Then, help students brainstorm different ways of making disturbances in the spring toy. Examples of different disturbances include pinching together some coils and letting them go, moving one end side to side, and moving one end up and down. Have students try some of these techniques in pairs and observe the results. Students should record their observations in writing or as sketches. Then have students compare the different types of waves they observed. If necessary, review the difference between longitudinal and transverse waves to help students make comparisons.

Answer Key

1. Accept all reasonable answers.

2. Accept all reasonable answers.
   Teacher Prompt What are some different ways you could cause disturbances in the spring toy? How will those disturbances affect the direction of the waves?

3. Answers will vary, but should include data to describe different types of disturbances and the effects of those disturbances on wave direction.
   Teacher Prompt Think about the question you asked in Step 1. What are you trying to learn? What data will help you get an answer to your question?

4. Answers will vary.

5. Sample answer: All the waves temporarily move the spring in some way. One type of wave moves the spring from side to side, while the other type of wave moves the spring forward and backward.

6. Sample answer: Waves could be classified based on whether the particles move parallel or perpendicular to the direction the wave travels.
   Teacher Prompt What is a transverse wave? What is a longitudinal wave? How do they differ from each other?

QUICK LAB INDEPENDENT *Inquiry*

Investigate Waves

In this lab, you will use a spring toy to investigate wave types. You will then compare the waves you observe and determine how to classify them.

PROCEDURE

1 With your partner, decide on a specific question to investigate that is related to wave direction. Consider the materials you have available, as well as time and space constraints. Record your question below.

_____

_____

_____

2 Describe a procedure that will allow you to investigate the question above.

_____

_____

_____

_____

_____

_____

_____

3 What data will you collect during your investigation?

_____

_____

_____

OBJECTIVE
- Differentiate between longitudinal and transverse waves.

MATERIALS
For each pair
- spring toy, coiled
For each student
- safety goggles

Quick Lab continued

4 With teacher approval, carry out your procedure. Record your data below.

5 Compare the waves you made. How are they alike? How are they different?

_____

_____

_____

_____

6 What criteria could you use to classify the waves you observed? Hint: Consider the difference between longitudinal and transverse waves.

_____

_____

_____

_____

QUICK LAB DIRECTED *Inquiry*

Water Waves GENERAL

👥 Large groups

🕐 15 minutes

LAB RATINGS

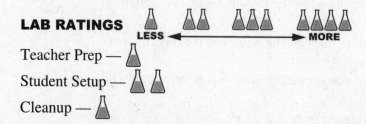

LESS ←——————→ MORE

Teacher Prep —

Student Setup —

Cleanup —

MATERIALS

For each group
- block, rectangular wood
- cooking trays, aluminum, deep
- cork
- water

For each student
- lab apron
- safety goggles

SAFETY INFORMATION

Remind students to review all safety cautions and icons before beginning this lab. Instruct students to clean up any water spills immediately as slippery floors can be dangerous.

TEACHER NOTES

In this activity, students will investigate how waves in water affect the motion of a floating object. Students will place a cork in a water-filled tray and form a hypothesis about how waves will move the cork. As one student moves a block in the water to create waves, the other students will observe and record the motion of the water and the cork. Students will then describe whether or not their results support their hypothesis. Have students take turns creating waves so that each student has an opportunity to observe the waves.

Tip Students may think of waves in lakes or oceans as movement of water rather than energy. This activity is designed to help students understand the difference between a wave and its medium.

Skills Focus Forming Hypotheses, Drawing Conclusions

MODIFICATION FOR GUIDED *Inquiry*

Instruct students to investigate how mechanical waves in water affect the motion of a floating object. Give students the materials to create wave tanks and have them form hypotheses and devise procedures to test their hypothesis. After you have approved their procedures, allow students to carry them out. Have students determine how to record their observations. Once all students have completed the activity, have them share their observations and conclusions with the class.

My Notes

_____

_____

_____

_____

_____

Quick Lab continued

Answer Key

3. Answers will vary. Make sure that students' hypotheses are testable and explanatory.

4. Description or sketch should explain that the cork remains in the same place as it bobs up and down.

5. Answers will vary, but students should explain why their hypothesis was supported or not supported by their results.

6. Waves transfer energy, not matter. Matter, in this case the water and the cork, returns to its original position once a wave has passed.
   Teacher Prompt What happened when you stopped creating waves in the tray? Did the cork move to a different location?

7. Sample answer: The waves we observed passed through a medium: water.
   Teacher Prompt What are characteristics of mechanical waves? What caused the waves?

8. Sample answer: Sound waves are mechanical waves that travel through the air. When we talk or play an instrument, sound waves travel through the air and can be heard by our ears.
   Teacher Prompt What kind of wave is produced when we talk? What medium do they travel through?

QUICK LAB DIRECTED *Inquiry*

Water Waves

In this lab, you will investigate how mechanical waves in a water-filled tray affect the medium they pass through. Remember that a mechanical wave is a wave that travels through a medium.

PROCEDURE

1 Fill the tray about halfway with water. Place a cork in the water near the center of the tray.

2 How will waves in the tray affect the motion of the cork? Discuss your ideas within your group.

3 Write a hypothesis to answer the question in Step 2. Explain your reasoning.

_____

_____

_____

_____

4 Choose one group member to move the block up and down in the water at one end of the tray to create waves. Observe the motion of the cork and the water. Describe or sketch your observations in the space below.

5 Do your results support the hypothesis that you made? Explain.

_____

_____

_____

_____

OBJECTIVES
• Distinguish between a wave and its medium.
• Describe properties and give examples of mechanical waves.

MATERIALS

For each group
• block, rectangular wood
• cooking trays, aluminum, deep
• cork
• water

For each student
• lab apron
• safety goggles

Quick Lab continued

6 Do waves transfer energy or matter? Explain.

_____

_____

_____

_____

7 How did the waves you observed show characteristics of mechanical waves?

_____

_____

_____

_____

8 Describe another example of a mechanical wave.

_____

_____

QUICK LAB DIRECTED *Inquiry*

Investigate Frequency GENERAL

👥 Small groups

🕐 30 minutes

LAB RATINGS

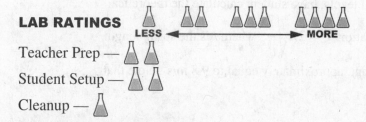

LESS ←————————————→ MORE

Teacher Prep —

Student Setup —

Cleanup —

MATERIALS

For each group
- marker
- metal washers, 3
- protractor
- ruler, metric
- stopwatch
- string, 1 meter (m)
- tape, transparent

For each student
- safety goggles

SAFETY INFORMATION

Remind students to review all safety cautions and icons before beginning this lab. Caution students to be careful that their swinging pendulum does not strike a student or another object.

TEACHER NOTES

In this activity, students will work in small groups to gain familiarity with the concepts of frequency and period by observing a simple pendulum. Begin with a description of general periodic motion, listing specific examples such as pendulums and ocean waves that can be similarly characterized by terms such as period, frequency, and amplitude.

Working in small groups, students will create a simple pendulum by tying three washers to a string taped to a desk edge. Students will run three trials at each of three different string lengths (i.e., they vary the period, holding amplitude constant). Using a stopwatch, they measure the period for 10 cycles and then convert the periods into frequencies in hertz (Hz). They will graph frequency against string length and note that frequency decreases with increasing string length.

Tip This activity focuses on frequency; another in the series covers wavelength. Both concepts will be used in the unit lab.

Skills Focus Practicing Lab Techniques, Making Graphs

My Notes

_____

_____

_____

_____

_____

Quick Lab continued

MODIFICATION FOR GUIDED Inquiry AND FOR INDEPENDENT Inquiry

After the introduction, provide students with materials suitable for building pendulums. Instruct them to make pendulums and to devise a way to vary frequency and to graph the results. For an extended independent activity, instruct students to use the pendulums to investigate the effect of amplitude on frequency or period. (Frequency and period should be independent of amplitude.) As an option at all levels, have student calculate the theoretical period at each string length, given by the equation $T = 2\pi\sqrt{\dfrac{l}{g}}$, where l is the string length in meters (m) and g is the gravitational constant, approximately equal to 9.8 m/s^2. Note that amplitude does not appear in the formula.

Answer Key

9. Check the student charts.

11. Sample answer: The longer the string, the lower the frequency.

12. Sample answer: The swinging string is like the disturbance of a wave. They are both periodic motion. It is similar to a wave in that it has frequency and amplitude.

13. Sample answer: It differs from a wave in that it does not transfer energy from one place to another.

QUICK LAB **DIRECTED** *Inquiry*

Investigate Frequency

Motion that repeats in equal time intervals is periodic motion. Examples include vibrating guitar strings, a weight bouncing up and down at the end of a spring, and swinging pendulums. In this lab, you will work in a small group to investigate frequency by building and observing a pendulum in periodic motion.

OBJECTIVES

- Build and use a pendulum.
- Relate the pendulum motion's period to its frequency.
- Relate pendulum string length to frequency.

MATERIALS

For each group:
- marker
- metal washers, 3
- protractor
- ruler, metric
- stopwatch
- string, 1 meter (m)
- tape, transparent

For each student
- safety goggles

PROCEDURE

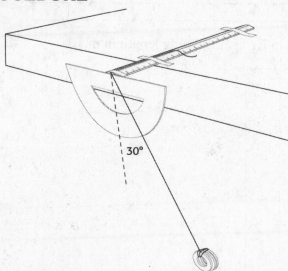

30°

1 Tie the three washers onto one end of the string.

2 Use the marker to mark the string at 0.2, 0.4, and 0.6 m from the center of the washers.

3 Tape the ruler to the desk so that it hangs 10 cm over the edge.

4 Tape the string along the ruler so that the 0.2 m mark is at the end of the ruler and the string hangs freely down over the end.

5 For each trial, divide the tasks so that one person holds the protractor and places the washers in the starting position, and another person operates the stopwatch. Start the pendulum at 30 degrees from vertical, and then move the protractor away to avoid interfering with the string.

6 Use the stopwatch to measure the time required for 10 complete swings of the pendulum from 30 degrees and back. Record your data below to the nearest tenth of a second(s). Run three trials at each string length.

7 Find the average time for 10 cycles for each string length to the nearest tenth of a second. Record the average times in the table.

Quick Lab continued

8 Divide by 10 to find the average period T, the time for one cycle, for each string length. Record the average periods in the table.

9 Take the reciprocal of the periods, or 1/T, to find the average frequency in cycles per second for each string length. Cycles per second is also the unit of hertz, abbreviated Hz. Record the average frequencies in the table below.

String length, m	Time for 10 cycles, s			Average time for 10 cycles, s	Average Period T = time for one cycle, s	Average Frequency 1/T, cycles/s or Hz
	Trial 1	Trial 2	Trial 3			
0.2						
0.4						
0.6						

10 Use the blank graph to record frequency in Hz against string length in m.

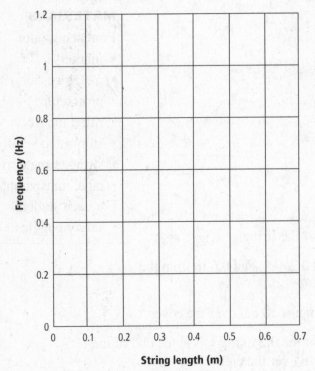

11 How did changing the length of the string affect the frequency?

_____

12 How is a swinging pendulum like a wave?

_____

13 How is a swinging pendulum different from a wave?

_____

QUICK LAB DIRECTED Inquiry

Waves on a Spring GENERAL

👥 Small groups

🕐 30 minutes

LAB RATINGS

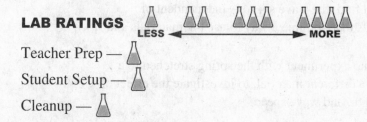

LESS ⟵——————⟶ MORE

Teacher Prep —

Student Setup —

Cleanup —

MATERIALS

For each group
- meterstick
- spring toy, coiled
- stopwatch
- tape, masking

For each student
- safety goggles

SAFETY INFORMATION

Remind students to review all safety cautions and icons before beginning this lab. Remind students to keep control of both ends of the coiled spring toy while performing the lab.

TEACHER NOTES

In this activity, students use a spring toy to investigate the relationships among wave speed, frequency, and wavelength. Students place a spring coil toy on the floor or table and stretch it out to a length of 3 meters (m). They will mark the placement of the ends with masking tape.

The students first determine the wave speed by flicking a pulse down the spring and measuring the time required for the wave to travel to the other end and back. They perform three trials and take the average. This is a good time to make the point that the wave speed is dependent on the medium the wave travels in.

Then students use the spring to set up a standing wave with a wavelength equal to the distance marked off with tape. They measure the time required for 10 cycles and calculate the frequency, again taking the average of three trials.

Finally, with the average wavelength, average wave speed, and average frequency found in the activity, students attempt to discover the mathematical relationship among them (wave speed = wavelength times frequency).

Tip This activity ties together the concepts of frequency, wavelength, and average wave speed. The optional activities demonstrate what wave speed is <u>not</u> dependent upon.

Skills Focus Practicing Lab Techniques, Drawing Conclusions

My Notes

_____

_____

_____

_____

_____

Quick Lab continued

MODIFICATION FOR GUIDED *Inquiry*

Have students develop a hypothesis about the relationship between wavelength and wave frequency. Students should use the list of materials to develop a set of procedures to test their hypothesis. Allow students to proceed with all reasonable experiments.

If time permits, students may also investigate the effect of different amplitudes and wavelengths on the wave speed. (They should find that wave speed is independent of amplitude and wavelength.) Direct the students to determine a way to use the materials and the type of data they will collect.

If time permits, students may also repeat the experiment with the spring stretched to a different length, or with a spring toy made of a different material, to investigate the effect of changing the medium on frequency, wavelength, and wave speed.

Answer Key

2. Sample answer: The wave pulse traveled down the coil. When it reached the end, it reflected back, traveling to the opposite side. The wave appeared to lose some energy as it went along since the amplitude was less by the time the pulse returned.

3. Accept all reasonable answers.

4. Accept all reasonable answers.

5. Sample answer: The medium for the waves is the coiled spring. We could alter the medium by holding it at a different length, changing the tension. We could use springs made of different materials or that were wound differently.

9. Answers will vary. The values should match those found and recorded in the tables, and include units.

10. Correct forms of the equation: speed = wavelength × frequency; wavelength = speed ÷ frequency; frequency = speed ÷ wavelength.

Waves on a Spring

Different waves, from ocean waves to sound waves to electromagnetic waves, can be described by their frequency, wavelength, and wave speed. In this activity, you will use a coiled spring toy to investigate the relationships between these three factors.

PROCEDURE

1 Place the coil spring toy on a table or on the floor and stretch it out to a length of 3 meters (m). Mark the placement of the ends with masking tape. Record the length of the spring in the table below.

2 Use the masking tape to mark a spot 30 cm to one side of the spring. Two students hold the ends of the spring at the places marked by the tape. One person holds an end firmly in place. The second person snaps the other end rapidly to the piece of masking tape on the side and back, sending a transverse wave pulse down the spring. Carefully observe the motion of the wave, especially its behavior at the end held firmly in place. Describe the wave motion.

_____

_____

_____

3 Again, hold the ends of the spring in place at the two points marked by the tape and send a transverse wave pulse down the spring. Use the stopwatch to measure the time required for the wave to travel to the firm end and back. Record the time in the table below. Perform three trials as consistently as possible and take the average.

OBJECTIVE

- Determine the mathematical relationships between the wavelength, frequency, and speed of a wave.

MATERIALS

For each group
- meterstick
- spring toy, coiled
- stopwatch
- tape, masking

For each student
- safety goggles

WAVE SPEED DATA

Trial	Length of spring, m	Time for wave, s	Speed of wave, m/s
1			
2			
3			
Average			

4 Use the values for length and times that you recorded earlier to calculate the wave speed for each trial. Remember that the distance the wave travels is twice the spring length. Find the average wave speed for the three trials and enter it into the table.

Quick Lab continued

⑤ The wave speed is dependent on the properties of the medium. What is the medium for the waves in this activity? How could you alter this medium?

_____

⑥ Again, hold the ends of the spring in place at the two points marked by the tape. Have one person move the spring from side to side to the masking tape to create a standing wave that looks like this:

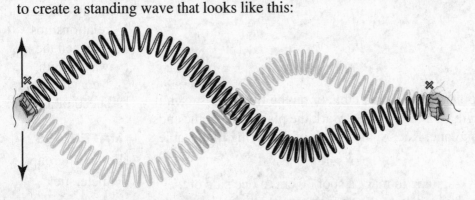

The wavelength of this standing wave is the distance between the tape marks, or 3 m.

⑦ Measure the time required for 10 cycles of the wave pattern. (One back-and-forth shake is one cycle.) Try to be consistent. Keep the pattern going long enough to complete three trials. Record your data in the table below.

FREQUENCY DATA

Trial	Time for 10 cycles, s	Wave frequency, Hz
1		
2		
3		
Average		

⑧ Calculate the wave frequencies, and take the average of three trials.

⑨ Find the values for the average wave speed (from Step 4) and average frequency (from Step 7). Copy them and the wavelength (from Step 6) here. Include the units.

_____

_____

_____

⑩ Analyze the mathematical relationship among these three quantities. Multiply or divide any two of them to see if the result equals the third. Using the terms *wavelength, frequency,* and wave *speed,* write the equation that shows the relationship.

_____

EXPLORATION LAB GUIDED *Inquiry* **AND** INDEPENDENT *Inquiry*

Investigate Wavelength GENERAL

👥 Small groups
🕐 45 minutes

LAB RATINGS

LESS ◄─────────► MORE

Teacher Prep —

Student Setup —

Cleanup —

MATERIALS

For the class
- cleanup materials, such as a broom and dustpan or towels

Note: These are suggested materials for the students to choose from in building their pendulums. They or you may come up with other materials from the classroom or home that could be used.

For each group
- balloon
- bottle, plastic (1)
- construction paper sheets, colored (12)
- glue
- graduated cylinder, 50 or 100 mL
- meterstick
- paper, graphing
- sand, fine
- scissors
- stopwatch
- string
- tape
- white paper (½ sheet)

For each student
- lab apron
- safety goggles

SAFETY INFORMATION

Remind students to review all safety cautions and icons before beginning this lab. Have a broom and dust pan available for spilled sand.

TEACHER NOTES

In this activity, students will work in small groups to gain familiarity with the concept of wavelength by building and observing a simple pendulum. Students will use a pendulum releasing a stream of sand over a moving strip of paper, or similar apparatus, to create a position-time graph. The students will measure the wavelengths of the graphs created and will investigate the effect of varying pendulum string lengths on wavelength.

Begin by explaining to the students that the motion of swinging pendulums is periodic, and can be characterized by terms such as period, frequency, and amplitude. Note that the position of a moving pendulum over time traces out a waveform, with a specific wavelength related to the period of oscillation and the length of the pendulum.

For the guided inquiry, provide a selection of suitable materials and instruct the students to investigate wavelength using a pendulum of variable lengths swinging over a moving paper strip to create a position-time graph. The students will decide how to use these materials to create a setup that can demonstrate wavelength; you will approve the proposal for safety at the planning stage and may make suggestions. Students will develop and document a repeatable testing procedure for using the pendulum, record data such as time and distance measurements, and describe the motion of their apparatus. Students will run two trials at three different pendulum string lengths to investigate the effect on wavelength.

Exploration Lab continued

For the independent inquiry, instruct the students to find a way to create a position-time graph of a swinging pendulum of variable length in order to investigate wavelength. The students will decide how to create a setup that can demonstrate wavelength; approve the proposal for safety at the planning stage and make suggestions as appropriate. For example, students may choose to create a pendulum from a swinging water bottle leaking a stream of water, and walk with it along a sidewalk outside the building, measuring wavelength from the water marks on the pavement. Instruct students to develop and document a repeatable testing procedure for using the pendulum to record data such as time and distance measurements and to describe the motion of their apparatus.

Tip A swinging pendulum has readily observable characteristics of period/frequency and amplitude, as explored in another lab in this series. This activity brings in the concept of wavelength.

Skills Focus Developing Procedures, Building Experimental Setups, Drawing Conclusions

MODIFICATION FOR DIRECTED Inquiry

To modify the lab for directed inquiry, provide specific directions on the construction of the pendulum and the use of a moving paper strip to trace out the waveform, as well as datasheets for the trials.

Answer Key for GUIDED Inquiry

DEVELOP A PLAN

1. Sample answer: Our pendulum will be a string with a swinging balloon dispensing sand from a small hole onto a moving strip of gluey paper. One person will hold the string and operate the pendulum. A second person will pull the paper under the swinging pendulum. A third person will use the stopwatch to help the paper person always pull at the same speed. We will practice the speed of the paper before we use it with the pendulum. Once we have the waveform traced out on the paper with the sand, we will use the meterstick to measure the wavelength. For each trial we will record the string length, the wavelength, and also the time for at least three cycles of the pendulum.

FORM A HYPOTHESIS

2. Sample answer: If I increase the length of the string on a pendulum, then the wavelength traced out on the paper will <u>increase</u> because <u>I know that frequency decreases with increasing string length, and frequency is inversely proportional to wavelength.</u>

ANALYZE THE RESULTS

5. Sample answer: The swinging pendulum did trace out a waveform, but at first the balloon let out too much sand and we had to start over. It was also hard to keep it swinging straight. Eventually we did get at least one good trial at each of three string lengths.

My Notes

6. Sample answer: The wavelength increased with increasing string length.

7. Sample answer: (The graph should show that wavelength increases with increasing string length.)

DRAW CONCLUSIONS

8. Sample answer: The pendulum lab data did support my hypothesis. Wavelength did increase when the string length was longer.

9. Sample answer: At first the balloon let too much sand out because the hole was too big, but then we used another balloon and reinforced it with tape before we made the hole. That worked better. Our results were pretty repeatable between trials, so our setup seemed to work well.

Connect TO THE ESSENTIAL QUESTION

10. Sample answer: The time that a pendulum takes to complete one back-and-forth cycle is its period in seconds per cycle. The inverse of that, or the number/fraction of cycles it completes per second, is its frequency in Hertz. The distance that the pendulum swings from the vertical, or the distances away from the centerline of the waveform peaks on the position-time graph, is its amplitude. The distance from peak to peak along the position-time graph is its wavelength.

Answer Key for INDEPENDENT Inquiry

DEVELOP A PLAN

1. Sample answer: Our pendulum will be a string with a swinging balloon dispensing sand from a small hole onto a moving strip of gluey paper. One person will hold the string and operate the pendulum. A second person will pull the paper under the swinging pendulum. A third person will use the stopwatch to help the paper person always pull at the same speed. We will practice the speed of the paper before we use it with the pendulum. Once we have the waveform traced out on the paper with the sand, we will use the meterstick to measure the wavelength. For each trial we will record the string length, the wavelength, and also the time for at least three cycles of the pendulum.

FORM A HYPOTHESIS

2. Sample answer: If I increase the length of the string on a pendulum, then the wavelength traced out on the paper will <u>increase</u> because <u>I know that frequency decreases with increasing string length, and frequency is inversely proportional to wavelength.</u>

ANALYZE THE RESULTS

5. Sample answer: The swinging pendulum did trace out a waveform but at first the balloon let out too much sand and we had to start over. It was also hard to keep it swinging straight. Eventually we did get at least one good trial at each of three string lengths.

6. Sample answer: The wavelength increased with increasing string length.

7. Sample answer: (The graph should show that wavelength increases with increasing string length.)

DRAW CONCLUSIONS

8. Sample answer: The pendulum lab data did support my hypothesis. Wavelength did increase when the string length was longer.

9. Sample answer: At first the balloon let too much sand out because the hole was too big, but then we used another balloon and reinforced it with tape before we made the hole. That worked better. Our results were pretty repeatable between trials, so our setup seemed to work well.

Connect TO THE ESSENTIAL QUESTION

10. Sample answer: The time that a pendulum takes to complete one back-and-forth cycle is its period in seconds per cycle. The inverse of that, or the number/fraction of cycles it completes per second, is its frequency in Hertz. The distance that the pendulum swings from the vertical, or the distances away from the centerline of the waveform peaks on the position-time graph, is its amplitude. The distance from peak to peak along the position-time graph is its wavelength.

EXPLORATION LAB GUIDED *Inquiry*

Investigate Wavelength

A swinging pendulum demonstrates periodic motion; it is easy to observe its period, or time for each cycle, and its amplitude. Less obvious is that the position of the pendulum over time traces out a waveform, which can be analyzed to determine wavelength. In this activity, you will build a pendulum and construct a position-time graph of its motion to find its wavelength.

OBJECTIVE
- Explore the concept of wavelength in periodic motion.

MATERIALS
For each group
- items provided by your teacher to choose from in building your setup
- meterstick
- paper, graphing
- stopwatch
For each student
- lab apron
- safety goggles

PROBLEM

How does changing the length of a pendulum change the length of the waves it makes?

PROCEDURE

DEVELOP A PLAN

1 Working with your group, review the materials provided by your teacher and develop a plan for building and using your testing setup. Make sure it meets the following requirements:

- The setup must include a swinging pendulum and a strip of paper moving under the pendulum at right angles to the plane of its motion.
- There must be a way for the pendulum's back-and-forth position to be recorded on the strip of paper as they both move.
- You have a plan for measuring the wavelength of the graph created on the paper.
- Be sure that you can easily change the pendulum's length to three different positions.
- The paper's motion will be fairly smooth, constant, and the same for each trial.
- You have a repeatable testing procedure for using the pendulum.
- You have a plan for recording relevant data.

  On a separate piece of paper, draw your proposed setup and describe how you plan to use it. Have your teacher approve the plan before continuing.

FORM A HYPOTHESIS

2 Complete the hypothesis sentence below:

If I make the length of the string on a pendulum longer, then the wavelength traced out on the paper will _____ because _____

_____

_____

Exploration Lab continued

BUILD A MODEL

❸ Work with your group to gather materials and build your setup.

TEST THE HYPOTHESIS

❹ Follow your plan to use the setup. Run at least two trials at each string length. Use the blank table below or a separate sheet to record your data. You may not need all the columns or rows provided, or you may collect more data than the table has space for.

WAVELENGTH OF A SWINGING PENDULUM

Trial	String length, m			

ANALYZE THE RESULTS

❺ **Describing Events** Describe what happened during your testing.

_____

_____

_____

_____

❻ **Recognizing Patterns** Look for and describe patterns in your data.

_____

_____

_____

❼ **Constructing Graphs** Graph your results on a separate sheet of paper. Use the string length on the *x*-axis and the wavelength on the *y*-axis.

DRAW CONCLUSIONS

8 **Evaluating Hypotheses** Was your hypothesis supported by your data? Discuss why or why not.

_____
_____
_____

9 **Evaluating Methods** Did the testing setup and procedure work well to investigate the wavelength of a swinging pendulum? What changes would you make to improve the testing plan?

_____
_____
_____

Connect TO THE ESSENTIAL QUESTION

10 **Identifying Concepts** Explain how the motion of a swinging pendulum can be described in terms of the properties of a wave, including period, frequency, amplitude, and wavelength.

_____
_____
_____
_____
_____
_____
_____

EXPLORATION LAB INDEPENDENT *Inquiry*

Investigate Wavelength

A swinging pendulum demonstrates periodic motion; it is easy to observe its period, or time for each cycle, and its amplitude. Less obvious is that the position of the pendulum over time traces out a waveform, which can be analyzed to determine wavelength. In this activity, you will build a pendulum and construct a position-time graph of its motion to find its wavelength.

PROBLEM

How does changing the length of a pendulum change the length of the waves it makes?

PROCEDURE

DEVELOP A PLAN

❶ Working with your group, develop a plan for building a setup that can create a position-time graph of a swinging pendulum of variable length. Make sure it meets the following requirements:

- The setup must include a swinging pendulum and produce some kind of a record over time of its back-and-forth position.
- You have a plan for measuring the wavelength.
- Be sure that you will be able to easily change the pendulum's length to different positions.
- You have a repeatable testing procedure for using the pendulum.
- You have a plan for recording relevant data.

On a separate piece of paper, draw your proposed setup and describe how you plan to use it. Have your teacher approve the plan before continuing.

FORM A HYPOTHESIS

❷ Complete the hypothesis sentence below:

If I make the length of the string on a pendulum longer, then the wavelength of the pendulum's motion on a position-time graph will _____ because _____

_____.

BUILD A MODEL

❸ Work with your group to gather materials and build your setup.

OBJECTIVE

- Explore the concept of wavelength in periodic motion.

MATERIALS

For each group
- items identified and collected by your group for building your setup
- meterstick
- paper, graphing
- stopwatch

For each student
- lab apron
- safety goggles

Exploration Lab continued

TEST THE HYPOTHESIS

❹ Follow your plan to use the setup. Run at least two trials at each string length. Use the blank table below or a separate sheet to record your data. You may not need all the columns or rows provided, or you may collect more data than the table has space for.

WAVELENGTH OF A SWINGING PENDULUM

Trial	String length, m				

ANALYZE THE RESULTS

❺ **Describing Events** Describe what happened during your testing.

_____

_____

_____

_____

❻ **Recognizing Patterns** Look for and describe patterns in your data.

_____

_____

❼ **Constructing Graphs** On a separate piece of paper, graph your results. Use the string length on the *x*-axis and the wavelength on the *y*-axis.

DRAW CONCLUSIONS

❽ **Evaluating Hypotheses** Was your hypothesis supported by your data? Discuss why or why not.

_____

_____

Exploration Lab continued

9 **Evaluating Methods** Did the testing setup and procedure work well to investigate the wavelength of a swinging pendulum? What changes would you make to improve the testing plan?

_____

_____

_____

Connect **TO THE ESSENTIAL QUESTION**

10 **Identifying Concepts** Explain how the motion of a swinging pendulum can be described in terms of the properties of a wave, including period, frequency, amplitude, and wavelength.

_____

_____

_____

_____

_____

_____

_____

_____

QUICK LAB DIRECTED *Inquiry*

Investigate Sound Energy GENERAL

👥 Student pairs
⏱ 20 minutes

LAB RATINGS

LESS ◄——————————► MORE

Teacher Prep —
Student Setup —
Cleanup —

MATERIALS

For each pair
• balloon, round
• jar, clear glass
• pencil (with eraser)
• rubber band
• salt
• scissors

For each student
• safety goggles

SAFETY INFORMATION

Remind students to review all safety cautions and icons before beginning this lab. Students should handle the glass jars carefully to avoid breakage and should use care when stretching the balloon over the mouth of the jar.

TEACHER NOTES

In this activity, students will investigate how sound waves travel through a medium. They will place salt in the bottom of a jar and stretch a balloon across the top of the jar. They will use a pencil eraser to tap the stretched balloon, and observe the behavior of the salt in response to the tapping. From these observations, students will form a hypothesis about how sound waves travel and will brainstorm another method that could be used to test the hypothesis.

Tip Circulate as students assemble the material to make sure they are tightly stretching the balloon. If students have difficulty seeing the salt move in the bottom of the jar, have them place a few grains of salt on the top of the balloon stretched over the mouth of the jar and repeat their experiments.

Skills Focus Forming Hypotheses, Making Observations

MODIFICATION FOR GUIDED *Inquiry*

Begin by posing a question to students, such as "How do sound waves travel?" Tell students that they will use the materials provided to investigate the answer to that question, but challenge them to devise their own procedure. Circulate among students as they work and offer suggestions for assembling the materials if needed.

My Notes

_____
_____
_____
_____
_____

Answer Key

5. Sample answer: The salt vibrates and moves a little bit when we tap the balloon with the pencil eraser.

6. Accept all reasonable answers. Students should understand that the vibrating balloon causes the salt to vibrate. This demonstrates that the energy of vibration has traveled from one place to another.

7. Accept all reasonable answers. The salt would not vibrate because there would be no medium (air) to transfer the waves. However, some students may believe that the salt would still vibrate because the sound waves could travel through the glass. Accept either answer.

8. Sample answer: Sound waves travel as waves of particle vibrations because they require physical substances in order to be transmitted.

9. Accept all reasonable answers. Students should develop a way to test the idea that sound requires a medium through which to travel.

Investigate Sound Energy

In this lab, you will make a simple apparatus to observe the effects of sound energy on salt crystals. You'll use your observations of the way the salt moves to form a hypothesis about sound waves. You'll then work with your partner to brainstorm another way you could test your hypothesis.

PROCEDURE

❶ Sprinkle several grains of salt into the jar. Place the jar on a flat surface in a well-lit spot.

❷ Use the scissors to cut off the neck of the balloon.

❸ Stretch the balloon over the mouth of the jar and pull the sides down past the rim of the jar's mouth. Work with your partner to wrap a rubber band around the balloon and the neck of the jar. Make sure the balloon fits tightly over the jar. See the image below for details.

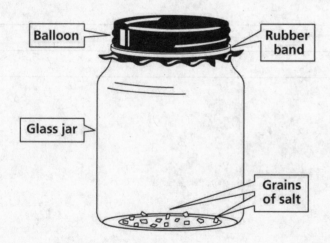

Balloon
Rubber band
Glass jar
Grains of salt

❹ Tap the balloon with the eraser end of the pencil. Make careful observations of what happens to the salt on the bottom of the jar.

❺ What happened to the salt when you tapped the balloon?

_____

_____

OBJECTIVES

• Observe how sound waves travel through a medium.

• Describe properties of waves.

MATERIALS

For each pair
• balloon, round
• jar, clear glass
• pencil (with eraser)
• rubber band
• salt
• scissors

For each student
• safety goggles

Quick Lab continued

6 How do you explain what you observed?

_____

_____

7 Suppose you could pump all of the air out of the jar and could leave the salt grains in the jar with the tightly stretched balloon on top. If you repeated this experiment, do you think the results would be different? How? Explain your answer.

_____

_____

_____

8 Work with your partner to develop a hypothesis to explain how sound travels. Remember that hypotheses are testable "because" statements.

_____

_____

9 Work with your partner to develop a way to test your hypothesis. Your procedure should be different from the methods used in this lab. Write your idea below.

_____

_____

_____

Different Instrument Sounds GENERAL

👥 Small groups

🕐 30 min

LAB RATINGS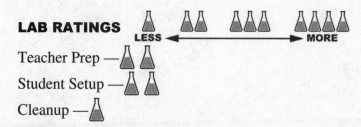

Teacher Prep —

Student Setup —

Cleanup —

MATERIALS

For each group
• pencil
• rubber band, thick (2)
• rubber band, thin (2)
• shoebox

For each student
• safety goggles

SAFETY INFORMATION

Remind students to review all safety cautions and icons before beginning this lab.

TEACHER NOTES

In this activity, students will explore the relationships between tension and length when producing sounds from a handmade student instrument. Students will report on the means by which an instrument can be manipulated to produce varying sounds as well as explore the fundamental properties of waves. Provide the students with shoeboxes, rubber bands of different thicknesses, and pencils.

Awareness of terms such as *pitch*, *note*, and *volume* may vary considerably among students. Consider sharing vocabulary to describe sounds as the class works through Steps 1–15 so that students can establish a shared vocabulary based on experience.

Expand the activity by challenging groups of 6–8 students to create music that features melodies made of notes of different pitches as well as rhythms based on repeating patterns of sounds.

Teacher Tip This activity may help students understand the relationship between loudness and amplitude.

Skills Focus Making Observations, Identifying Relationships

MODIFICATION FOR GUIDED *Inquiry*

Allow students to suggest and test their own materials to use as strings on the shoebox. Before testing each material, students should develop a hypothesis about the kind of sound the material will make, and how that sound is related to the properties of the material. Students should develop a table of materials that successfully produce sounds and should use their observations to reject or accept their hypothesis.

My Notes

_____

_____

_____

_____

_____

Quick Lab continued

Answer Key

1. Answers may vary.

2. Answers may vary.

3. Sample answer: The sounds are different: one rubber band sounds lower and the other rubber band sounds higher.

5. Sample answer: The sound is higher.

6. Sample answer: The length is shorter.

8. Sample answer: The sound is lower.

9. Sample answer: The length is greater.

10. Answers may vary.

11. Answers may vary.

14. Answers may vary.

16. Sample answer: The harder the rubber band is plucked, the louder the sound is.

17. Sample answer: The thicker the rubber band is, the lower the pitch.

18. Sample answer: The shorter the rubber band is, the higher the pitch.

Different Instrument Sounds

In this lab, you will model the way that different instruments make sound by listening to and observing the sounds different materials make when strung across a shoebox and plucked.

PROCEDURE

1 Stretch a **rubber band** lengthwise around an empty **shoebox**. Place the box hollow side up. Pluck the rubber band gently. Describe what you hear.

_____

_____

_____

2 Stretch another rubber band of a different thickness around the box. Pluck the rubber band gently. Describe what you hear.

_____

_____

_____

3 Pluck both rubber bands at the same time. Describe what you hear.

_____

_____

_____

4 Put a **pencil** across the center of the box and under the rubber bands, and pluck the thin rubber band again.

5 Describe how the sound has changed since Step 1.

_____

_____

_____

_____

OBJECTIVES

- Observe how different materials produce different types of sound.
- Describe the relationship between the structure of a material and the sound it produces.

MATERIALS

For each group
- pencil
- rubber band, thick (2)
- rubber band, thin (2)
- shoebox

For each student
- safety goggles

Quick Lab continued

6 Describe how the length of vibrating rubber band has changed since Step 1.

_____

_____

_____

7 With the pencil in the same location, pluck the thick rubber band.

8 Describe how the sound has changed since Step 2.

_____

_____

9 Describe how the length of vibrating rubber band has changed since Step 2.

_____

_____

10 Move the pencil closer to one end of the shoebox. Pluck on both rubber bands and on both sides of the pencil.

11 Describe how the four sounds compare to each other.

_____

_____

_____

_____

_____

_____

12 Remove the rubber bands, and put two of the same thickness on the box.

13 Experiment with placing the pencil across the center of the box to create four different sounds when the rubber bands are plucked.

14 Describe how you arranged the pencil on the box.

_____

_____

_____

_____

Quick Lab continued

15 Pluck the rubber bands gently and then more forcefully.

16 Describe the relationship between how hard you plucked and the sound you heard.

_____

_____

17 Describe the relationship between the thicknesses of the rubber bands and the sounds you hear.

_____

_____

_____

_____

_____

18 Describe the relationship between the vibrating length of the rubber band and the sounds you hear.

_____

_____

_____

_____

_____

_____

QUICK LAB DIRECTED *Inquiry*

Investigate Loudness GENERAL

👥 Student pairs
🕐 20 minutes

LAB RATINGS

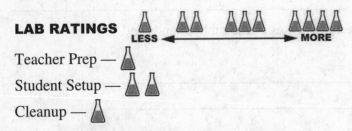

LESS ◄─────────► MORE

Teacher Prep — 🍶

Student Setup — 🍶 🍶

Cleanup — 🍶

SAFETY INFORMATION

Remind students to review all safety cautions and icons before beginning this lab. Students should use caution when cutting the cardboard because thick materials can be difficult to cut.

TEACHER NOTES

In this activity, student pairs will use a piece of cardboard and a rubber band to produce sounds of different amplitudes. They will make predictions about what they will hear. From this they will understand that the loudness of a wave is directly related to its amplitude.

Tip Some students may find it helpful to view a pre-made model of the cardboard and rubber band. If you think any of your students may struggle with the concepts in this lab, prepare a sample to have on hand for students to use as a guide in constructing their own model.

Student Tip Think of the rubber band as a guitar string that produces a sound wave. What happens to the loudness of the sound when the rubber band is pulled higher on the cardboard?

Skills Focus Forming Prediction, Practicing Listening, Making Observations

MODIFICATION FOR GUIDED *Inquiry*

Students can complete the lab as assigned, but with additional challenges. After they have produced the two sounds, ask them how they could produce sounds of higher or lower amplitude. You can also extend the lesson by challenging students to produce a difference in pitch. In this case, students should alter the placement of the pencils.

MATERIALS

For each pair
• cardboard
• marker
• pencil (2)
• rubber band (large)
• ruler, metric
• scissors

For each student
• safety goggles

My Notes

_____

_____

_____

_____

_____

Answer Key

4. Sample answer: I think the rubber band will make a louder sound when it is stretched to the four-centimeter mark.

7. Sample answer: The sound was louder when the rubber band was pulled to the four-centimeter line than when it was pulled to the one-centimeter line.

8. Accept all reasonable answers.

9. Accept all reasonable answers. Students should understand that loudness and amplitude are directly related; the higher the amplitude of a sound wave, the louder the sound produced by that wave.

10. Sample answer: Hitting the drumstick harder would make a louder sound because the skin on the drum head would vibrate with a higher amplitude.

   Teacher Prompt What will happen to the amplitude of the sound waves when the drum is hit softly? How will that amplitude change when the drum is hit harder?

QUICK LAB DIRECTED Inquiry

Investigate Loudness

In this lab, you will investigate the relationship between the amplitude of a sound wave and the loudness of the sound it produces. Remember that the amplitude of a wave is measured by the maximum height of that wave. You and your partner will stretch a rubber band across a piece of cardboard and pluck it to produce sounds of different amplitudes.

PROCEDURE

① Cut a notch in the middle of both ends of the cardboard. Stretch the rubber band around the cardboard so that it fits into the notches.

② Measure and mark one-centimeter lines on the cardboard. Measure from the length of the stretched rubber band. Label the one-centimeter line and the four-centimeter line.

③ Slide the pencils under the rubber band at each end. Your piece of cardboard should look like the below image.

OBJECTIVE
• Understand the relationship between amplitude and loudness.

MATERIALS
For each pair
• cardboard
• marker
• pencil (2)
• rubber band (large)
• ruler, metric
• scissors
For each student
• safety goggles

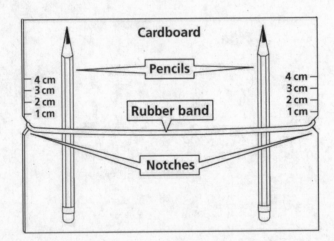

④ Make a prediction about what will happen to the loudness when you pull the rubber band to different heights (different amplitudes).

_____

_____

⑤ Pull the rubber band to the one-centimeter line and let it go so that it vibrates with low amplitude. Listen carefully to the sound it makes.

Quick Lab continued

6 Pull the rubber band to the four-centimeter line and let it go. This time the amplitude is higher. Listen carefully to the sound it makes.

7 How did the loudness of the two sounds compare?

_____

_____

8 Was your prediction correct? If not, revise it below to reflect what actually occurred.

_____

_____

9 How is amplitude related to loudness?

_____

_____

10 Using what you learned from this experiment, explain why swinging a drumstick harder on a drum would make a louder sound than swinging the drumstick lightly.

_____

_____

EXPLORATION LAB DIRECTED Inquiry **AND** GUIDED Inquiry

Sound Idea ADVANCED

👥 Small groups
🕐 45 minutes

LAB RATINGS

LESS ◄────────────► MORE

Teacher Prep —

Student Setup —

Cleanup —

MATERIALS

For each group
• cup, plastic
• eraser, pink rubber
• rubber band
• tuning fork, different frequency (1)
• tuning forks, same frequency (2)
• water

For each student
• safety goggles

SAFETY INFORMATION

Remind students to review all safety cautions and icons before beginning this lab. Paper towels should be available to clean up spilled and/or splashed water.

TEACHER NOTES

In this activity, students will explore sound as the transfer of energy by vibrations in a medium. They will use tuning forks and simple materials to discover that while sounds can possess many unique characteristics, all sounds transfer energy from one place to another. If you would like to demonstrate the difference between the waves produced by tuning forks with two different pitches, place a piece of plastic wrap over the top of a plastic cup or beaker, holding it in place with a rubber band. Sprinkle a very small pinch of sand or salt onto the plastic wrap. Place the eraser on the table and tap it with one of the tuning forks, then hold it horizontally 1 cm above the plastic wrap. Repeat with the other frequency tuning fork and note the differences. The higher frequency fork will produce more "jumping" (vibration) of the particles.

Tip If students struggle with their results in Steps 8–11 in the Directed Inquiry lab (Steps 7–10 in Guided Inquiry), instruct them to first conduct the experiment with the tuning forks of the same frequency, and then repeat with two tuning forks of different frequencies.

Student Tip Think about how the energy required to make a sound can produce different frequencies.

Skills Focus Forming Hypotheses, Developing Procedures, Making Observations

My Notes

_____

_____

_____

_____

_____

MODIFICATION FOR INDEPENDENT Inquiry

Have students research and develop a testable hypothesis about the relationship between sound and energy. Students should write a procedure and list of materials for testing their hypothesis. Allow students to conduct all reasonable experiments.

Answer Key for DIRECTED Inquiry

ASK A QUESTION

1. Accept all reasonable answers.

MAKE OBSERVATIONS

4. Sample answer: The water moves away from the tuning fork in waves.

FORM A HYPOTHESIS

5. Accept all reasonable answers. Students should see that the water is a medium through which the sound waves travel.

6. Accept all reasonable answers.

TEST THE HYPOTHESIS

10. Sample answer: The second tuning fork is making the same sound.
Teacher Prompt Are the frequencies of the tuning forks the same or different? How will that affect the sound?

11. Accept all reasonable answers.

12. Accept all reasonable answers.

ANALYZE THE RESULTS

13. Sample answer: Even though energy is transferred though the air when a tuning fork is hit, it only causes another tuning fork to vibrate if the sound vibrations are at the same frequency as the tuning fork that wasn't struck.

DRAW CONCLUSIONS

14. Accept all reasonable answers.

15. Sample answer: It takes energy to move the windows to cause them to rattle. Therefore, energy from the thunder's sound waves must be transferred through the air to the windows.
Teacher Prompt What is the medium (or media) through which the thunder will travel?

Connect TO THE ESSENTIAL QUESTION

16. Sample answer: The louder sounds, like the sound when the first tuning fork was hit by the eraser, had more energy than the quieter sounds, like the sound produced by the second tuning fork.

Answer Key for GUIDED Inquiry

ASK A QUESTION

1. Accept all reasonable answers.

MAKE OBSERVATIONS

4. Sample answer: The water moves away from the tuning fork in waves.

FORM A HYPOTHESIS

5. Accept all reasonable answers. Students should see that the water is a medium through which the sound waves travel.

6. Accept all reasonable answers.

DEVELOP A PLAN

7. Accept all reasonable answers.
   Teacher Prompt How will your experiment use all three tuning forks? If you have difficulty deciding how to use the rubber band, try wrapping it around the prongs of one of the tuning forks and hitting it against the eraser. What happens and how can you use this in your experiment?

8. Accept all reasonable answers.
   Teacher Prompt Are there variables that you will not be able to control? If so, how might that affect your experiment?

9. Accept all reasonable answers.

MAKE OBSERVATIONS

10. Accept all reasonable answers.

ANALYZE THE RESULTS

11. Accept all reasonable answers.

DRAW CONCLUSIONS

12. Accept all reasonable answers.

13. Sample answer: It takes energy to move the windows to cause them to rattle. Therefore, energy from the thunder's sound waves must be transferred through the air to the windows.
   Teacher Prompt What is the medium (or media) through which the thunder will travel?

Connect TO THE ESSENTIAL QUESTION

14. Sample answer: The louder sounds, like the sound when the first tuning fork was hit by the eraser, had more energy than the quieter sounds, like the sound produced by the second tuning fork.

EXPLORATION LAB DIRECTED Inquiry

Sound Idea

In this lab, you will explore how sound made by a tuning fork carries though different materials. You will first create a hypothesis about the relationship between sound and energy, and then test your hypothesis by doing simple experiments.

PROCEDURE

ASK A QUESTION

1 No matter what type of sound we hear and regardless of what causes the sound, all of the sounds we hear share a common element. In this lab, you will investigate the following question: What do all sounds have in common? Explain.

_____

_____

_____

MAKE OBSERVATIONS

2 Fill the plastic cup with water.

3 Lightly strike a tuning fork on the eraser. Carefully place the prongs of the tuning fork in the water without touching the sides of the plastic cup.

4 What happens? Record your observations below.

_____

_____

_____

_____

FORM A HYPOTHESIS

5 Just as it takes energy to produce a sound, sound transfers energy from one place to another through vibrations in a medium. Explain how this relates to your observations.

_____

_____

_____

OBJECTIVES

• Describe the properties of sound waves.

• Understand that all sound requires a medium in which to travel.

MATERIALS

For each group

• cup, plastic

• eraser, pink rubber

• rubber band

• tuning fork, different frequency (1)

• tuning forks, same frequency (2)

• water

For each student

• safety goggles

Exploration Lab continued

6 Write a hypothesis about the relationship between sound and energy transfer. Your hypothesis should incorporate your observations and the information in Step 4. It should be a testable, "because" statement.

_____

_____

7 Review the rest of these lab instructions. If you cannot test your hypothesis using these activities, rewrite your hypothesis so that it can be tested.

TEST THE HYPOTHESIS

8 Strike a tuning fork on the eraser. Quickly pick up a second tuning fork with the same frequency in your other hand and hold it about 5 cm away from the first tuning fork.

9 Place the first tuning fork against your leg to stop the tuning fork's vibration. Listen closely to the second tuning fork.

10 Record your observations, including the frequencies of the two tuning forks.

_____

_____

11 Repeat Steps 8–10, using the remaining tuning fork (with a different frequency) as the second tuning fork. Record your observations in the space below.

_____

_____

12 Use the two tuning forks that have the same frequency and place a rubber band tightly over the prongs near the base of one tuning fork. Strike both tuning forks against the eraser. Hold the bases of the tuning forks against a table, 3–5 cm apart. If you cannot hear any differences, move the rubber band up or down the prongs and strike again. Record you observations about the differences in the sounds you heard.

_____

_____

Exploration Lab continued

ANALYZE THE RESULTS

13 **Comparing Events** You used turning forks of different frequencies in Steps 8–10. Explain how the results compared the two times you followed the procedure.

_____

_____

_____

_____

DRAW CONCLUSIONS

14 **Examining Observations** Did the results of your tests support your hypothesis? Why or why not?

_____

_____

_____

15 **Analyzing Models** Particularly loud thunder can cause the windows of your room to rattle. How is this evidence that sound waves carry energy?

_____

_____

_____

Connect TO THE ESSENTIAL QUESTION

16 **Describing Concepts** Describe the different sounds you heard during this experiment. What do the differences in sound tell you about the energy of those sound waves?

_____

_____

_____

EXPLORATION LAB GUIDED (Inquiry)

Sound Idea

In this lab, you will explore how sound made by a tuning fork carries though different materials. You will first create a hypothesis about the relationship between sound and energy, and then test your hypothesis by doing simple experiments.

PROCEDURE

ASK A QUESTION

❶ No matter what type of sound we hear and regardless of what causes the sound, all of the sounds we hear share a common element. In this lab, you will investigate the following question: What do all sounds have in common? Explain.

_____

_____

_____

MAKE OBSERVATIONS

❷ Fill the plastic cup with water.

❸ Lightly strike a tuning fork on the eraser. Carefully place the prongs of the tuning fork in the water without touching the sides of the plastic cup.

❹ What happens? Record your observations below.

_____

_____

_____

FORM A HYPOTHESIS

❺ Just as it takes energy to produce a sound, sound transfers energy from one place to another through vibrations in a medium. Explain how this relates to your observations.

_____

_____

_____

OBJECTIVES
- Describe the properties of sound waves.
- Understand that all sound requires a medium in which to travel.

MATERIALS
For each group
- cup, plastic
- eraser, pink rubber
- rubber band
- tuning fork, different frequency (1)
- tuning forks, same frequency (2)
- water

For each student
- safety goggles

Exploration Lab continued

6 Write a hypothesis about the relationship between sound and energy transfer. Your hypothesis should incorporate your observations and the information in Step 4.

_____

_____

_____

_____

DEVELOP A PLAN

7 In the space below, describe an experimental setup and procedures that will allow you to test your hypothesis. You should use all of the materials that are associated with this lab.

_____

_____

_____

_____

_____

8 What variables will you control in your experiment? How will you control them?

_____

_____

_____

9 Identify the data you will collect during your experiment. Make sure to identify what you will observe and how you will record your observations.

_____

_____

_____

_____

Exploration Lab continued

MAKE OBSERVATIONS

10 Show your proposed procedure to your teacher. Once you have received approval, carry out your experiment. Record your observations below. Include either a sketch or a table of your data.

_____

_____

_____

_____

_____

_____

ANALYZE THE RESULTS

11 **Evaluating Methods** Evaluate your experimental setup and procedure. Did it allow you to make the observations you needed to answer the question? Were there variables that you did not control that may have affected your results? Describe any modifications you would make if you were to repeat the experiment. If time allows, repeat the experiment with your modifications and record the new results.

_____

_____

_____

_____

_____

DRAW CONCLUSIONS

12 **Examining Observations** Did the results of your tests support your hypothesis? Why or why not?

_____

_____

_____

Exploration Lab continued

13 **Analyzing Models** Particularly loud thunder can cause the windows of your room to rattle. Explain how this is evidence that sound waves carry energy.

_____

_____

_____

_____

Connect **TO THE ESSENTIAL QUESTION**

14 **Describing Concepts** Describe the different sounds you heard during this experiment. What do the differences in sound tell you about the energy of those sound waves?

_____

_____

_____

QUICK LAB DIRECTED *Inquiry*

Resonance in a Bottle GENERAL

👥 Small groups

🕐 15 minutes

LAB RATINGS

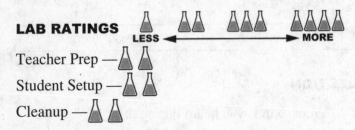

LESS ←——————→ MORE

Teacher Prep —

Student Setup —

Cleanup —

MATERIALS

For each group
- beaker
- bottle, glass
- ruler
- tuning forks, different pitches (2)
- water

For each student
- safety goggles

My Notes

_____

_____

_____

_____

_____

SAFETY INFORMATION

Remind students to review all safety cautions and icons before beginning this lab. Remind students to never strike the tuning fork on a hard object or on any part of their bodies. Warn students not to touch the beaker with the tuning fork.

TEACHER NOTES

In this activity, students will observe resonance between a vibrating tuning fork and a vibrating column of trapped air. When the tuning fork and column of air vibrate at the same frequency, the sound of the tuning fork will be noticeably louder. As students pour water into the bottle, they will probably exceed the resonant point. If this happens, have students pour some water back out of the bottle.

Skills Focus Making Observations, Identifying Relationships

MODIFICATION FOR GUIDED *Inquiry*

Have students think about how sound is produced. Pass out the tuning forks, and have students explore ways to produce sound with the tuning forks. Have students think about how another material, such as air, could produce the same sound. How could they produce this sound using a glass bottle, water, and air? Have students write out and test a set of procedures. Encourage students to relate the amount of air vibrating in the glass bottle to the frequency of the pitch. How is this similar to other musical instruments?

Answer Key

2. Sample answer: The air column resonates at the same frequency as the tuning fork, so the sound is louder.

3. Answers will vary.

4. Answers will vary.

5. Sample answer: The higher the frequency, the shorter the air column.

QUICK LAB DIRECTED *Inquiry*

Resonance in a Bottle

In this lab, you will explore how sound is produced by vibrating materials. First, you will observe the sound produced by a vibrating tuning fork, and then you will observe how a bottle of air and water responds to the tuning fork vibrations.

PROCEDURE

1 Strike the **tuning fork** on the floor, and hold it 1 cm above the **glass bottle**.

2 Gradually pour in **water** from the **beaker** until the sound of the tuning fork is much louder. Adjust the amount of water until the sound is the loudest. Why do you think the sound gets louder?

_____

_____

_____

_____

_____

_____

_____

_____

_____

_____

_____

_____

_____

3 Measure the length of the air column with a **ruler**. Record your measurement.

_____

OBJECTIVES

• Describe how sound is produced and affected by vibrations in a material.

MATERIALS

For each group
• beaker
• bottle, glass
• ruler
• tuning forks, different pitches (2)
• water

For each student
• safety goggles

4 Repeat the process with a different tuning fork. Is the frequency of the second tuning fork higher or lower than the first? Record the new length of the air column.

_____

_____

_____

_____

_____

_____

5 What is the relationship between the length of the resonating air column and the frequency of the tuning fork?

_____

_____

_____

_____

_____

_____

_____

_____

_____

_____

_____

_____

_____

_____

QUICK LAB **DIRECTED** *Inquiry*

The Speed of Sound GENERAL

👥 Large groups
🕐 20 minutes

LAB RATINGS

LESS ⟵————————⟶ MORE

Teacher Prep —
Student Setup —
Cleanup —

MATERIALS

For each group
• stopwatch (3)
• tape measure

My Notes

_____

_____

_____

_____

_____

TEACHER NOTES

In this activity, students will go outside and measure a field. They will split into two groups and measure how long it takes sound to travel the distance of the field. From these measurements they will compute the distance that sound travels each second.

Tip While some students are observing the stopwatches, other students also observe the time and record the second that each word reaches their ears. This will help student groups as they compute the average time it takes each word to travel the length of the field.

Student Tip When you are recording the amount of time it takes a sound to travel the length of the field, remember that the opposite group is yelling their word once every five seconds. During the experiment, have the stopwatches evenly spread out among your group.

Skills Focus Making Predictions, Recording Measurements

MODIFICATION FOR GUIDED *Inquiry*

To teach this lab at a higher level, challenge students to devise their own methods to compute the speed of a sound as it travels across a field rather than following the steps outlined in the procedures below. Students should take their own measurements (both of the field and of the time it takes for sound to travel the field) then use those measurements to compute the time it took for the sound to travel.

Answer Key

1. Sample answer: I predict that the sound will take three seconds to travel the length of the field. One challenge we may encounter is making sure everyone in the group agrees with the times shown on the stopwatch.

2. Accept all reasonable answers.

8. Sample answer:

Length of field (m)	Time for word to travel (seconds)	Distance sound traveled per second (m/s)
90 m	1.5 seconds	60 m/s

9. Accept all reasonable answers.

10. Accept all reasonable answers. Students should devise simple experiments that can test how quickly sound travels through water and through solids.

11. Accept all reasonable answers.

12. Sample answer: The speed of sound is different in different states of matter because of the space between the particles. In a solid the particles are close together, so the vibrations from the sound waves can travel quickly. There is more space between particles in a liquid, so sound waves travel more slowly through a liquid than a solid. Sound travels slowest in gases because of the very large spaces between particles.

13. Accept all reasonable answers. Students should understand that on a hot day, there will be even more space between the particles in the air than on a very cold day. The sound will travel faster on a cold day than on a warm day.

    Teacher Prompt Students may question this if they have observed that sound sometimes travels very slow on very cold days. You can explain that humidity can affect the speed of sound. On very cold days the air might be very dry compared to a very hot and humid day. The water particles in the very humid air will increase the density of the air, which causes sound to travel faster.

QUICK LAB DIRECTED Inquiry

The Speed of Sound

In this lab, you will work with your group to make a prediction about
how sound will travel over a large area. You'll then go outside and
send a sound across a field to the other group. They will record how
long it takes for the sound to reach their ears. From these data, you'll
figure out how quickly the sound traveled through air.

PROCEDURE

1 In this experiment, you will test how long it takes sound to
travel across a field. Before you go outside, make a prediction
about what you think will happen as you test the speed of
sound traveling across the field. How long will it take? What
challenges might you encounter?

_____

_____

_____

_____

2 With your group, decide on a word that you will call out during the
experiment. It should be a one-syllable word that will be easy to yell
quickly and loudly. The word "Hey!" will work, but your group may
also select another appropriate word to use. Write the word your group
selects on the line below.

_____

3 Go outside and use the tape measure to record the length of the field. Record
the data in the table below.

4 Line up on one end of the field. The other group will be on the opposite
end of the field. Your group will either be recording time or yelling a word
(your teacher will give you these instructions).

5 Your teacher will stand in the center of the field. When his or her arm drops,
begin your assigned task. If you are yelling a word, yell the word loudly and
quickly every five seconds. Use your stopwatch to keep track of the seconds
and to know when to yell. Repeat six times, for a total of 30 seconds.

OBJECTIVE

• Determine the
  speed of sound
  as it travels
  through air.

MATERIALS

For each group
• stopwatch (3)
• tape measure

Quick Lab continued

6 If you are timing, start the timer at your teacher's command and time how long it takes the first word to reach you. Continue for 30 more seconds, or until you have heard the other team's word six times. Record how long it took for the word to reach your side of the field. All members of your group should help figure out the time it took for the sound to travel. How many seconds did it take before the first word reached your ears? How many seconds did it take for the second word to reach your ears? Find the average time it took for all six words to reach your ears. Record your data in the table below.

7 Switch roles. If you were yelling a word during the first round, you will now use the timers to see how long it takes sound to travel the length of the field. If you were recording time, you will now yell a word to the other group.

8 Once the table is filled out, compute how long it took for sound to travel the length of the field. Then compute how far the sound traveled each second.

Length of field (m)	Time for word to travel (seconds)	Distance sound traveled per second (m/s)

9 Was your prediction correct? If not, revise it to reflect what actually happened.

_____

_____

10 Sound travels fastest though solids, slower in liquids, and still slower in gases. This experiment showed how sound travels through gases. How could you test the two other ways sound travels (through solids and through liquids)? Devise a sample experiment.

_____

_____

_____

_____

_____

_____

Quick Lab continued

11 What are the likely results of your above experiments?

_____

_____

_____

12 Why does the speed of sound depend on the matter through which it
is traveling?

_____

_____

_____

13 If all other variables are the same, how could the results of this experiment
differ between a very hot day and a very cold day? Explain your answer.

_____

_____

_____

_____

S.T.E.M. LAB GUIDED **Inquiry** AND INDEPENDENT **Inquiry**

Echoes GENERAL

👥 Small groups
🕐 45 minutes

LAB RATINGS

LESS ◄─────────────────► MORE

Teacher Prep —

Student Setup —

Cleanup —

MATERIALS

For each group
• aluminum foil
• can, coffee
• cardboard
• clay, modeling
• cloth
• corks
• egg carton, foam
• foam board
• horn
• mirror, plane
• pan, aluminum pie
• paper towels
• plastic tube
• plastic wrap
• plate
• scissors
• sponge

For each student
• safety goggles

SAFETY INFORMATION

Remind students to review all safety cautions and icons before beginning this lab. As each group will be working with a variety of different materials, they should be cautioned about any potential hazards that come with those materials (such as sharp edges, heavy weight, etc).

TEACHER NOTES

In this activity, students will test different materials and determine whether the materials reflect or absorb sound waves. Then, groups will use the results of their tests to aid in the design of a model or prototype to either echo sounds or reduce echoes. In the Guided Inquiry option, students will build a model of soundproofing material to absorb sound or a simple SONAR device to reflect sound. In the independent inquiry option, students will build a prototype of their own design and specifications to reflect or absorb sound. In both levels, students will brainstorm real-life uses for their designs. Students will test their models or prototype devices by creating a loud sound and observing what happens to the sound waves. The materials list specifies a horn, but any instrument or tool that creates a loud burst of sound is acceptable. Students will use their observations about sound to create hypotheses about how sound waves can travel and interact with matter. Both levels of the lab will end with questions to help students apply their understandings of sound and how it travels and interacts with different materials.

Tip Because several groups will be testing how different materials reflect or absorb sound waves, you might have greater success if this lab is completed outside. This will minimize sound overlap between groups.

Student Tip To learn more about how sound waves interact with matter, pay attention to other groups as they are testing models or prototypes.

Skills Focus Designing Prototypes, Forming Hypotheses, Making Observations

My Notes
_____
_____
_____
_____
_____

S.T.E.M. Lab continued

MODIFICATION FOR DIRECTED *Inquiry*

Assign each group just two materials to test. One material should absorb sound, such as foam, while the other material should reflect sound, such as the pie pan. After determining how their material interacts with sound waves, groups decide if they should use their material to build a soundproofing device or a sound-reflecting device. They can draw a sketch of their proposed design and explain the difference between sound reflection and sound absorption.

Answer Key for GUIDED *Inquiry*

ASK A QUESTION

1. Accept all reasonable answers.

DEVELOP A PLAN

2. Accept all reasonable answers. In general, students should devise a method to test whether sound waves are reflected or absorbed by different materials. They may do this by creating a loud sound, and have members of the group stationed at different distances away from the material to observe what happens to the sound waves. Accept any reasonable plan that students devise.

MAKE OBSERVATIONS

4. Accept all reasonable answers.
   Teacher Prompt How do you know if a material reflected or absorbed sound? Were there some materials that reflected sound better or absorbed sound better than other materials?

5. Accept all reasonable answers.

FORM A HYPOTHESIS

6. Sample answer: Sound is affected by the hardness of a surface.

7. Accept all reasonable answers.

BUILD A MODEL

8. Accept all reasonable answers. Students should write down that they will either be constructing soundproofing material or a simple SONAR-type device.

9. Accept all reasonable answers. Encourage students to use more than one material so that they can innovate as they construct their models.

TEST THE HYPOTHESIS

12. Accept all reasonable answers.

13. Sample answer: We tested a SONAR-type device which did support my hypothesis because sound waves require a hard surface to create an echo. When the sound from the horn hit the aluminum coffee can and pie plate model, it produced an echo.

S.T.E.M. Lab continued

ANALYZE THE RESULTS

14. Accept all reasonable answers.

15. Sample answer: Hard materials produced better echoes (reflect sound) than soft materials. Soft materials absorbed sound best. We also noticed that some models had irregular shapes. These models reflected some sound but didn't produce much of an echo.

DRAW CONCLUSIONS

16. Accept all reasonable answers.

17. Accept all reasonable answers.

Connect TO THE ESSENTIAL QUESTION

18. Sample answer: Echoes are caused when sound waves are reflected off an object and they reach our ears again. Not all materials produce an echo.

Answer Key for INDEPENDENT Inquiry

ASK A QUESTION

1. Accept all reasonable answers.

DEVELOP A PLAN

2. Accept all reasonable answers. In general, students should devise a method to test whether sound waves are reflected or absorbed by different materials. They may do this by creating a loud sound and have members of the group stationed at different distances away from the material to observe what happens to the sound waves. Accept any reasonable plan that students devise.

MAKE OBSERVATIONS

3. Accept all reasonable answers.

Teacher Prompt How do you know if a material reflected or absorbed sound? Were there some materials that reflected sound better or absorbed sound better than other materials?

4. Accept all reasonable answers.

FORM A HYPOTHESIS

5. Sample answer: Sound is affected by the hardness of a surface.

6. Accept all reasonable answers.

BUILD A PROTOTYPE

7. Accept all reasonable answers.

8. Accept all reasonable answers.

S.T.E.M. Lab continued

TEST THE HYPOTHESIS

11. Accept all reasonable answers.

12. Sample answers: My group tested an invention designed to make headphones quieter. It worked by adding soft material to the outside of the headphone set to make it absorb more sound. It supported my hypothesis because sound needs a hard surface to be reflected and because sound waves can't bounce off of soft surfaces. The invention did make the headphones sound quieter.

ANALYZE THE RESULTS

13. Sample answer: Hard materials produced better echoes (reflect sound) than soft materials. Soft materials absorbed sound best. We also noticed that some models had irregular shapes. These models reflected some sound but didn't produce much of an echo.

DRAW CONCLUSIONS

14. Accept all reasonable answers.

15. Accept all reasonable answers.

Connect TO THE ESSENTIAL QUESTION

16. Sample answer: Echoes are caused when sound waves are reflected off an object and they reach our ears again. Not all materials produce an echo.

S.T.E.M. LAB GUIDED Inquiry

Echoes

In this lab, you will test different materials and determine if they reflect sound or absorb sound. Then your group will build a model of either soundproofing material or SONAR (which is used to measure how sound reflects). You will test another group's model by creating a loud sound and observing how the model interacts with that sound. You'll form a hypothesis about sound waves and how they interact, and you'll apply your understandings about sound to your life.

PROCEDURE

ASK A QUESTION

❶ In this lab, you will investigate different ways sound waves can travel. Before you begin, think about how the same sound can behave differently depending on the location. Write about at least one example below. Name the locations, how the sound behaves in each, and why you think it behaves differently in the two locations.

_____

_____

_____

_____

DEVELOP A PLAN

❷ You will use the materials provided with this lab to experiment how sound waves can travel. With your group, look over the materials list and develop a plan to test them. What variables will you control, and how? Will you use the same steps to test each material? How will you record your results? Write your detailed plan below.

_____

_____

_____

_____

_____

_____

OBJECTIVES

• Identify an echo as a reflected sound wave.

• Design a device that either reflects or absorbs sound waves.

MATERIALS

For each group
• aluminum foil
• can, coffee
• cardboard
• clay, modeling
• cloth
• corks
• egg carton, foam
• foam board
• horn
• mirror, plane
• pan, aluminum pie
• paper towels
• plastic tube
• plastic wrap
• plate
• scissors
• sponge
For each student
• safety goggles

S.T.E.M. Lab continued

3 When you believe your plan is finished, show it to your teacher. When you have received approval for your plan, you may begin testing the different materials.

MAKE OBSERVATIONS

4 Which materials best absorbed sound wave? Which materials best reflected sound waves?

_____

_____

_____

_____

5 Create a table, sketch, or graph to display your results.

FORM A HYPOTHESIS

6 Why do you think certain materials are better at *reflecting* sound and other materials are better at *absorbing* sound? Use your observations from this lab in your answer.

_____

_____

_____

7 Form a hypothesis to explain how sound waves can interact with different materials. Your hypothesis should show an understanding of how sound waves travel, and it should be a testable "because" statement.

_____

_____

_____

S.T.E.M. Lab continued

BUILD A MODEL

8 Your group will now build a model of a device used to either reflect or absorb sound. Your teacher will assign you the model you will build. Half of the groups will build a model of a soundproofing device, used to keep rooms quiet and soundproof and absorb sound waves. The other half will build simple SONAR machines. SONAR is a machine that emits sound waves and measures the time it takes for the sound to return to its source. Write down which model your group will be constructing.

_____

9 How will you combine the materials you tested to build your model? Write down your plan.

_____

_____

_____

10 Build your model. Use as many materials as needed from the materials list, and keep in mind whether you want the sound to be reflected or absorbed.

TEST THE HYPOTHESIS

11 Your group will test the effectiveness of another group's model. Use the horn to create a loud sound, and carefully observe what happens.

12 Draw a picture to show what you think happened to the sound waves when it hit the model you tested.

13 How do these results support your hypothesis about how sound waves interact with other materials? If needed, revise your hypothesis.

_____

_____

_____

S.T.E.M. Lab continued

ANALYZE THE RESULTS

14 **Describing Results** What type of model did you test (sound-absorbing or sound-reflecting) and how did it perform when you aimed a loud sound at it? Explain why the model interacted the way it did with the sound waves.

_____

_____

_____

_____

15 **Interpreting Patterns** What quality makes a material a good sound reflector? What quality makes a material a good sound absorber?

_____

_____

_____

_____

DRAW CONCLUSIONS

16 **Evaluating Models** Which models designed to reflect sound were most successful and why? Which models designed to absorb sound were most successful and why?

_____

_____

_____

_____

17 **Applying Concepts** Work with your group to explain a situation from your life where a sound-reflecting device is important. Then, explain a situation from your life where a sound-absorbing device is important.

_____

_____

_____

_____

S.T.E.M. Lab continued

Connect TO THE ESSENTIAL QUESTION

⑱ **Explaining Concepts** Explain how echoes are caused. Use your understanding of sound waves from this lab.

_____

_____

_____

S.T.E.M. LAB INDEPENDENT *Inquiry*

Echoes

In this lab, you will test different materials and determine if they reflect sound or absorb sound. Then, your group will build a prototype of a device you invent to either reflect or absorb sound. You will test another group's prototype by creating a loud sound and observing how the prototype interacts with that sound. You'll form a hypothesis about sound waves and how they interact, and you'll apply your understandings about sound to your life.

PROCEDURE

ASK A QUESTION

1 In this lab, you will investigate different ways sound waves can travel. Before you begin, think about how the same sound can behave differently depending on the location. Write about at least one example below. Name the locations, how the sound behaves in each, and why you think it behaves differently in the two locations.

_____

_____

_____

_____

DEVELOP A PLAN

2 You will use the materials provided with this lab to experiment how sound waves can travel. With your group, look over the materials list and develop a plan to test them. What variables will you control, and how? Will you use the same steps to test each material? How will you record your results? Write your detailed plan below.

_____

_____

_____

_____

_____

_____

OBJECTIVES

- Identify an echo as a reflected sound wave.
- Design a device that either reflects or absorbs sound waves.

MATERIALS

For each group
- aluminum foil
- can, coffee
- cardboard
- clay, modeling
- cloth
- corks
- egg carton, foam
- foam board
- horn
- mirror, plane
- pan, aluminum pie
- paper towels
- plastic tube
- plastic wrap
- plate
- scissors
- sponge

For each student
- safety goggles

S.T.E.M. Lab continued

MAKE OBSERVATIONS

3 Which materials best absorbed sound wave? Which materials best reflected sound waves?

_____

_____

_____

_____

4 Create a table, sketch, or graph to display your results.

FORM A HYPOTHESIS

5 Why do you think certain materials are better at reflecting sound and other materials are better are absorbing sound? Use your observations from this lab in your answer.

_____

_____

_____

_____

6 Form a hypothesis to explain how sound waves can interact with different materials. Your hypothesis should show an understanding of how sound waves travel.

_____

_____

_____

_____

S.T.E.M. Lab continued

BUILD A PROTOTYPE

7 Work with your group to invent a machine that will be used to either reflect or absorb sound. Name your invention and start thinking about how to build a prototype of your invention. How will you combine the materials you tested to build your prototype?

_____

_____

_____

8 What will be the function of your invention? How will it be used?

_____

_____

_____

9 Build your prototype. Use as many materials as needed from the materials list, and keep in mind whether you want the sound to be reflected or absorbed.

TEST THE HYPOTHESIS

10 Your group will test the effectiveness of another group's prototype. Use the horn to create a loud sound and carefully observe what happens.

11 Draw a picture to show what you think happened to the sound waves when it hit the prototype you tested.

12 How do these results support your hypothesis about how sound waves interact with other materials? If needed, revise your hypothesis.

_____

_____

_____

S.T.E.M. Lab continued

ANALYZE THE RESULTS

⑬ Interpreting Patterns What quality makes a material a good sound reflector? What quality makes a material a good sound absorber?

_____

_____

_____

_____

⑭ Evaluating Models Which prototypes designed to reflect sound were most successful and why? Which models designed to absorb sound were most successful and why?

_____

_____

_____

_____

_____

DRAW CONCLUSIONS

⑮ Applying Concepts Work with your group to explain a situation from your life where a sound-reflecting device is important. Then, explain a situation from your life where a sound-absorbing device is important.

_____

_____

_____

_____

Connect TO THE ESSENTIAL QUESTION

⑯ Explaining Concepts Explain how echoes are caused. Use your understanding of sound waves from this lab.

_____

_____

_____

QUICK LAB DIRECTED Inquiry

QUICK LAB DIRECTED Inquiry

Making an AM Radio Transmitter BASIC

👥 Small groups

🕐 15 minutes

LAB RATINGS

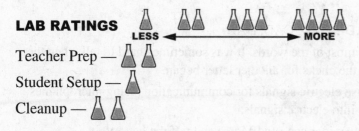

LESS ◄————————► MORE

Teacher Prep —

Student Setup —

Cleanup —

MATERIALS

For each group
• AM radio
• battery, 9-volt
• coin

For each student
• safety goggles

My Notes

_____

_____

_____

_____

_____

SAFETY INFORMATION

Remind students to review all safety cautions and icons before beginning this lab.

TEACHER NOTES

In this lab, students will build a basic AM radio transmitter, and then use it to send electrical signals to an AM radio receiver. Students will use a coin to bridge the terminals of a 9-volt battery to send a signal to an AM radio. The battery and AM radio must be only several centimeters apart from each other because the electrical signals are weak. Make sure the battery used is a fresh one. You may wish to try various coins to see if any particular type (copper, alloy, etc.) helps determine better performance.

Tip This activity will help students understand how sound is transmitted over long distances.

Student Tip When you listen to a radio, think about where the signals it receives come from.

Skills Focus Drawing Conclusions

MODIFICATION FOR INDEPENDENT Inquiry

Challenge students to make a basic AM radio transmitter that can send electrical signals. Provide students with a list of available materials. You may add additional materials such as lengths of wire, paper clips, nuts, bolts, and electrical tape. Have them create a plan for their transmitter to submit for your approval. Then have students make their transmitter. Ask students to provide written instructions that someone else could use to create a similar transmitter.

Answer Key

2. Sample answer: A clicking sound is heard on the AM radio receiver.
Teacher Prompt When you place the coin across the battery terminals, what do you hear?

3. Sample answer: By changing how long the coin stays in contact with the battery terminals, the length of the click can be shortened or lengthened.
Teacher Prompt What happens if you change how long the coin stays in contact with the battery?

4. Sample answer: FACE, FED, DEAF, FADE, FAD, CAD, DAB

5. Sample answer: We were able to decode most of the words. It was sometimes hard to tell when the clicks representing one letter ended, and the clicks for another letter began.

6. Sample answer: Telephones and radios use electric signals for communication, using microphones and mouthpieces to change sound waves into electric signals.

7. Sample answer: The battery-and-coin transmitter can send Morse code. If the battery was very powerful, it might signal the position of someone lost at sea or in a wilderness area.

8. Sample answer: Conventional telephones send and receive voice signals. We can also send a fax over a telephone line.

QUICK LAB DIRECTED *Inquiry*

Making an AM Radio Transmitter

In this lab, you will build a basic AM radio transmitter, and then use it to send electrical signals to an AM radio.

PROCEDURE

1 Tune the AM radio to a station where you can hear static.

2 Place the battery near the radio and bridge the battery terminals with the coin. What happens when you touch the coin to both terminals at the same time?

_____

3 Morse code is a method of sending messages using combinations of short and long tones, clicks, or lights to stand for different letters. How can you make both short and long clicks on your basic AM transmitter?

_____

_____

4 In this abbreviated key, a dot stands for a short click and a dash stands for a long click.

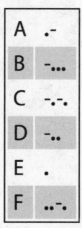

Have one person in your group create some short words using just the letters above (*e.g.*, CAB). The rest of the group should not see these words. The student will tap out the words using Morse code, while the rest of the group writes down the decoded words on the lines below.

_____

_____

<table>
<tr><td colspan="2">OBJECTIVES</td></tr>
<tr><td colspan="2">• Build an AM radio transmitter.</td></tr>
<tr><td colspan="2">• Send, receive, and decode AM radio signals.</td></tr>
<tr><td colspan="2">MATERIALS</td></tr>
<tr><td colspan="2">For each group</td></tr>
<tr><td colspan="2">• AM radio</td></tr>
<tr><td colspan="2">• battery, 9-volt</td></tr>
<tr><td colspan="2">• coin</td></tr>
<tr><td colspan="2">For each student</td></tr>
<tr><td colspan="2">• safety goggles</td></tr>
</table>

The abbreviated Morse code key:

A .-
B -...
C -.-.
D -..
E .
F ..-.

Quick Lab continued

5 Describe whether or not your attempt to use Morse code was successful. Explain what went well and what caused difficulties.

_____

_____

_____

6 How is this similar to the way a telephone works?

_____

_____

7 What important information could you send over the battery-and-coin transmitter?

_____

8 What information can you send using conventional telephone lines?

_____

Sound Recording and Playback GENERAL

👥 Small groups
🕐 25 minutes

LAB RATINGS

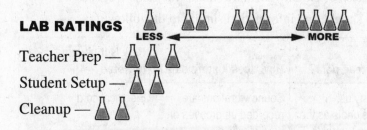

Teacher Prep —
Student Setup —
Cleanup —

MATERIALS

For each group
- computer station for Internet research

For each class
- cassette player and cassette tape
- CD player and CD
- MP3 player loaded with audio file(s)
- phonograph and vinyl record

SAFETY INFORMATION

Remind students to review all safety cautions and icons before beginning this lab.

TEACHER NOTES

In this activity, students will research and investigate various methods used for recording and playing back sound. Have students divide the tasks among members of the group to complete the table for each recording device. As long as music is played at a low level throughout the classroom, students will be able to observe the music from each station. Before class, you should collect the devices you are going to use, and make sure you have ample power outlets and/or batteries to power the devices.

Tip This activity will help students understand advances in the technology used to record and playback sound.

Student Tip Think about ways people use recorded sound in their daily lives.

Skills Focus Making Observations, Drawing Conclusions

My Notes

_____
_____
_____
_____
_____

MODIFICATION FOR INDEPENDENT Inquiry

Challenge students to identify and explore ways sound has been recorded and played back since 1877. Instruct them to create a poster that explains the history of four or five audio recording and playback devices, how the devices work, and the strengths and weaknesses of each. Have students give a demonstration of audio recording and playback using one the devices.

Answer Key

1. Sample answers: They all need a way to be powered, and they can all play back sounds. Some can also record and store lots of sounds. They are different in their size and in the various ways the sounds are stored. There are no fast-forward or rewind buttons on the phonograph.
   Teacher Prompt Are they all the same size? Do they all store sounds the same way?

2. Accept all reasonable answers. Students should find information similar to the following:

	When was it created?	How does it read data?	How does it store data?	How is it usually powered?
Phonograph	1877	A needle, or stylus, decodes the signals as the disc spins on a turntable.	Sound vibrations are recorded as grooves on a hard plastic disc.	Electrical cord
Cassette player	1963	The tapes are decoded by a magnetic head and turned into sound.	Sound is stored on a tape reel housed in a plastic casing.	Electrical cord or batteries
CD player	1969	A laser reads pits and produces an electric signal that is then converted into a sound wave.	Audio CDs digitally store information in a series of pits on the surface of the CD.	Electrical cord or batteries
MP3 player	1989	Software reads digital files and converts these files into sound.	Sound is stored as a digital file	Charged by connecting player to a USB port on computer

3. Accept all reasonable answers. Students should find information similar to the following:

	Strengths	Weaknesses
Phonograph	Easy to access any track on a record.	Phonograph records break and wear out easily. Needles frequently need to be replaced on phonographs.
Cassette player	Cassettes much easier to store than phonograph records. Easy to record new sounds.	Hard to get to beginning of a song.
CD player	Extremely portable.	Difficult to record sounds. CDs are not much smaller than cassettes. CDs can be scratched.
MP3 player	Extremely portable. Stores lots of sound files in device.	Loss of informational materials that used to come with CDs, cassettes, and records.

4. Sample answer: The devices are becoming smaller. They now have the ability to store all or much of the sound they play back in the device itself.

5. Accept all reasonable answers. Students should be able to express that improvements in the design and production of these devices are driven by what consumers want the devices to do. People want fast access to sound. Convenience is very important.

Sound Recording and Playback

In this lab, you will identify and explore ways sound can be recorded and played back.

PROCEDURE

1 With your teacher, have your entire class list ways sound can be recorded and played back. What do the different audio devices you listed have in common, and what is different about them?

_____

_____

_____

2 Use the Internet to research the following topics for each of the audio devices listed above. Record your findings in this table.

	When was it created?	How does it read data?	How does it store data?	How is it powered?
Phonograph				
Cassette player				
CD player				
MP3 player				

OBJECTIVES

- Investigate methods used for recording and playing back sound.
- Determine the strengths and weaknesses of various types of audio devices.

MATERIALS

For each group
- computer station for Internet research

For each class
- cassette player and cassette tape
- CD player and CD
- MP3 player loaded with audio file(s)
- phonograph and vinyl record

Quick Lab continued

❸ In small groups, take turns visiting each of the four stations and listen to a sample of a sound recording on each device. What conclusions can you draw about the strengths and weaknesses of each device? Record your observations in the table below.

	Strengths	Weaknesses
Phonograph		
Cassette player		
CD player		
MP3 player		

❹ You have studied how each of these audio devices work. What trends do you notice in the design of these devices?

_____

_____

_____

❺ Imagine you are planning the next generation of devices to record and play back sound. What forces do you think drive improvement in the design and production of audio equipment?

_____

_____

_____

QUICK LAB DIRECTED Inquiry

Investigate the Electromagnetic Spectrum GENERAL

👥 Small groups
🕐 20 minutes

LAB RATINGS

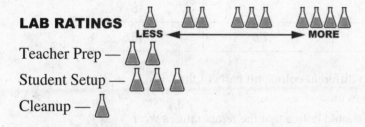

LESS ◄──────► MORE

Teacher Prep —

Student Setup —

Cleanup —

MATERIALS

For each group
• marker, black, washable
• paper, white blank
• prism
• prism stand or cardboard box
• tape
• thermometers (3)

For each student
• lab apron
• safety goggles

SAFETY INFORMATION

Remind students to review all safety cautions and icons before beginning this lab.

TEACHER NOTES

In this activity, students will measure temperature changes taking place in thermometers exposed to different regions of the visible light spectrum. Students will first paint the bulbs of each thermometer black. Then they will position the prism in a prism holder or attach it to the edge of a cardboard box in such a way as to spread the light spectrum onto a sheet of white paper. Next, students tape the thermometers together and position them on the paper so that each thermometer bulb is exposed to a different color of visible light. After five minutes, students will make temperature readings.

It is best to have students take an initial reading of each thermometer and compare that to the final reading after exposure to a specific color of visible light. Thermometers may not be calibrated exactly the same, making direct comparisons between thermometers difficult.

It also works well to use digital thermometers in place of traditional alcohol lab thermometers.

Tip At the end of the activity, students should notice a linear progression of temperatures.

Skills Focus Working Collaboratively, Practicing Lab Techniques, Drawing Conclusions

MODIFICATION FOR GUIDED Inquiry

Provide the materials and ask students to develop a procedure using those materials to determine whether all the colors of visible light yield the same temperature change.

My Notes

_____

_____

_____

_____

_____

Answer Key

3. Sample data:

SAMPLE TEMPERATURE DATA

	Color: RED	Color: GREEN/BLUE	Color: VIOLET
Initial Temperature (°C)	16	16	16
Final Temperature (°C)	18	17.5	16.5

5. Sample answer: The white light split into different colors; all parts of the electromagnetic spectrum are not visible to us.

6. Accept all reasonable answers. Students should notice that the temperatures were different and that they decreased in a linear progression from red to yellow to green to blue to violet.

7. Sample answer: When sunlight is separated into its components, each color of light is associated with a different amount of energy.

QUICK LAB DIRECTED *Inquiry*

Investigate the Electromagnetic Spectrum

In this lab, you will use a prism to separate sunlight into a color spectrum. Then you will measure temperature changes taking place in thermometers exposed to different regions of this spectrum.

PROCEDURE

1 First, use the marker to color the bulb of each thermometer black.

2 While the ink is drying, position the prism in a prism holder or attach it to the edge of a cardboard box under natural sunlight in such a way as to spread the light spectrum onto the white paper.

3 When the paint is dry, record the initial temperature of each thermometer in the table below.

TEMPERATURE DATA

	Color:	Color:	Color:
Initial Temperature			
Final Temperature			

4 Position the thermometers on the paper you prepared in Step 2 so that each thermometer bulb is exposed to light of a different color. Tape each in place. Wait five minutes. Then record the final temperature measurement of each thermometer in the data table.

OBJECTIVES

- Use a prism to separate the sun's light into visible colors.
- Determine whether exposure of thermometers to different colors of visible light result in different changes in temperature.
- Relate any changes observed to differences in the energy levels within the electromagnetic spectrum.

MATERIALS

For each group
- marker, black washable
- paper, white blank
- prism
- prism stand or cardboard box
- tape
- thermometers (3)

For each student
- lab apron
- safety goggles

Quick Lab continued

5 What did you notice in Step 2 when you allowed sunlight to pass through the prism?

_____

_____

6 What did you notice about the temperature when each thermometer was exposed to the different colors of visible light?

_____

_____

7 Heat is a type of energy. What can you infer from this activity about the energy associated with sunlight?

_____

_____

QUICK LAB   DIRECTED Inquiry

White Light   GENERAL

👥 Small groups
🕐 20 minutes

LAB RATINGS

LESS ←————————→ MORE

Teacher Prep —
Student Setup —
Cleanup —

MATERIALS

For each group
- electromagnetic spectrum diagram
- flashlight
- glass prism
- paper, construction (1 sheet)
- scissors
- tape

SAFETY INFORMATION

Remind students to review all safety cautions and icons before beginning this lab. Glass prisms may have sharp edges. Remind students to be careful when handling the prisms. Also, instruct students not to open the flashlight or handle the batteries.

My Notes

_____
_____
_____
_____
_____

TEACHER NOTES

In this activity, students will use a prism to demonstrate that white light is composed of all the visible colors in the electromagnetic spectrum. As light passes through a prism, each wavelength of light is refracted by a slightly different amount. The electromagnetic spectrum diagram you use with students should include the wavelengths and frequencies for the various colors of visible light.

Tip For best results, this activity should be done in a darkened room with powerful flashlights. Alternatively, this activity can be done outside using sunlight instead of a flashlight.

Skills Focus Making Observations, Conducting Research, Identifying Relationships

MODIFICATION FOR   GUIDED Inquiry

Instead of giving students the instructions for how to perform the activity, have them experiment with different setups and procedures. Students may choose to modify the amount of light that shines on the prism (by covering it with different amounts of construction paper) to investigate how this changes the refracted light, or they may investigate how the light refracts as it moves through multiple prisms. Have students write down the procedures they will follow. Then, allow students to carry out their investigations, being sure to record their observations. Have students take note of how much each color refracts through the prism. Encourage students to compare the pattern of refracted light with the colors of visible light in the electromagnetic spectrum. They should also compare the wavelengths of light with the amount the light is refracted.

Quick Lab continued

MODIFICATION FOR INDEPENDENT Inquiry

Have students choose a scenario to investigate. Have them brainstorm the different places they have seen rainbows or other color-separated light (in the sky after it rains, in an oil puddle, or when light shines through glass). Have students write down the materials they could use and procedures they could follow to model these situations. Then, allow students to carry out their investigations, being sure to record their observations. Have students take note of how much each color bends. Encourage them to compare the pattern of light with the colors of visible light in the electromagnetic spectrum. They should also compare the wavelengths of light with the amount the light bends.

Answer Key

4. Student diagrams should show that light enters on one side of the prism and exits on a different side, producing a rainbow. Their drawings should also show that violet light refracts more than red light does.

5. Sample answer: Red bends the least.
   Teacher Prompt Point to the angles in the student's illustration. Which color bends the least? [red]

6. Sample answer: Violet bends the most.
   Teacher Prompt Point to the angles in the student's illustration. Which color bends the most? [violet]

7. Sample answer: Yes, light with a shorter wavelength and higher frequency will refract more than light with a longer wavelength and lower frequency.

QUICK LAB DIRECTED *Inquiry*

White Light

In this lab, you will demonstrate how white light consists of different colors of light. You will shine a flashlight into a glass prism to observe how different colors of light change direction when they travel through glass.

PROCEDURE

1 Use **scissors** to cut a slit in a **piece of construction paper.** Tape the paper over the end of a **flashlight.**

2 Turn on the flashlight, and lay it on a table. Place a **prism** on end in the beam of light.

3 Slowly rotate the prism until you can see a rainbow on the surface of the table.

4 Draw a diagram of the light beam, the prism, and the rainbow.

OBJECTIVES

• Describe how white light consists of different colors of light.

MATERIALS

For each group
• electromagnetic spectrum diagram
• flashlight
• glass prism
• paper, construction (1 sheet)
• scissors
• tape

5 Which color of light bends the least?

_____

_____

_____

Quick Lab continued

6 Which color bends the most?

_____

_____

_____

_____

7 Research the wavelengths and frequencies of the colors you see in your rainbow. Are the wavelength and frequency of light related to how much the light bends? Explain.

_____

_____

_____

_____

_____

_____

_____

Why Is the Sky Blue? ADVANCED

👥 Small groups
🕐 15 minutes

LAB RATINGS

LESS ← → MORE

Teacher Prep —

Student Setup —

Cleanup —

MATERIALS

For each group
- flashlight or penlight, thin beam
- glue sticks, transparent hot melt type
- white background, paper or wall

For each student
- safety goggles

SAFETY INFORMATION

Remind students to review all safety cautions and icons before beginning this activity. Warn students not to shine the flashlight into their own eyes or the eyes of other students. Although glue sticks are non-toxic, remind students to avoid contact between the glue sticks and their mouth and clothing.

My Notes

TEACHER NOTES

In this activity, students will model the scattering of sunlight through the atmosphere by observing how light scatters when it travels through a glue stick. The white light emitted by a flashlight (and the sun) consists of different wavelengths of visible light that correspond to the different colors of light. Some wavelengths of light scatter more easily through materials than others. Blue, or short wavelength, light is more easily scattered by materials in the glue (and the sky) than red, or long wavelength, light. Because of this, the flashlight beam will appear yellow when it travels a short distance through the glue because the blue scatters more. (This is a model of how the sun appears yellow and the sky appears blue during the day.) When the flashlight beam travels a longer distance through the glue, more of the shorter wavelengths will begin to scatter, causing the beam to appear orange/red. (This is a model of how the sun and sky appear orange/red at sunset. During sunset, the sun is lower in the sky, and sunlight must travel a longer distance through the atmosphere before reaching an observer.)

Tip If you have only regular, full-sized flashlights available, try making masks to block the excess light. Trace the lens of the flashlight on black paper. Then, center the glue stick on the paper and trace the diameter of the glue stick. Cut out the doughnut-shaped mask, and place it over the lens of the flashlight. This activity works best in a dimly lit room.

Skills Focus Making Models, Making Observations, Applying Concepts

Quick Lab continued

MODIFICATION FOR GUIDED Inquiry

Have students think about how they could use a flashlight and glue stick to model the path of sunlight through Earth's atmosphere. Have students consider the path of sunlight through the atmosphere at noon, and have them consider the path at sunset. When does sunlight travel a shorter distance, and when does it travel a longer distance? How are the colors of the sun and sky different at these times? Have students brainstorm a set of procedures to investigate the path of sunlight at these different times. Encourage students to record all observations. How does the light look when it travels through the glue stick? What color is the light after it travels through the glue stick? How does this model explain the color of the sun and sky at different times of the day?

Answer Key

1. Sample answer: white

2. Sample answer: The glue stick appears blue. The beam on the white surface appears yellow.

3. Sample answer: The part of the glue stick closest to the light source appears blue. All colors of light appear along the length of the glue stick. The beam of light on the white surface appears orange-red.

4. Sample answer: The light beam appeared yellow when it traveled through a short length of glue, and it appeared orange-red when it traveled through a longer length of glue.

5. Sample answer: The sky looks blue during the day because blue light scatters when it travels a short distance through the atmosphere. During sunset, the light travels farther through the atmosphere, so all of the blue light is scattered from the sun. This causes the sun to appear orange-red.

   Teacher Prompt Think about how far sunlight travels when it is directly overhead at noon. How far does it travel when the sun is setting? How do the light waves from the flashlight traveling through the different lengths of glue sticks represent the light waves from the sun traveling through the atmosphere?

QUICK LAB DIRECTED *Inquiry*

Why Is the Sky Blue?

In this lab, you will investigate how light scatters by creating a model of the sun and Earth's atmosphere. You will use a flashlight to represent the sun and a glue stick to represent Earth's atmosphere.

PROCEDURE

1 Shine a **flashlight** onto a **white surface**, such as a wall or a sheet of paper. What color is the light?

_____

_____

_____

2 Hold a **glue stick** perpendicular to the flashlight, and shine the light into the center of the glue stick. What color do you see on the glue stick? What color is the light beam on the white surface?

_____

_____

_____

_____

_____

3 Now place the light against one end of the glue stick, and shine the light through the length of the glue stick. What color does the glue stick appear closest to the light source? What colors do you observe as the light travels along the glue stick from the light source? What color is the light beam on the white surface?

_____

_____

_____

_____

_____

_____

_____

OBJECTIVES

• Describe the scattering of light through materials.

MATERIALS

For each group
• flashlight or penlight, thin beam
• glue sticks, transparent hot melt type
• white background, paper or wall

For each student
• safety goggles

Quick Lab continued

4 How did the thickness of the glue stick affect the color of the beam on the white surface?

_____

_____

_____

_____

_____

_____

5 How can this model explain why the sky looks blue when the sun is directly overhead at noon? How does it explain why the sun appears orange-red during sunset?

_____

_____

_____

_____

_____

_____

_____

_____

_____

_____

_____

_____

_____

_____

_____

QUICK LAB DIRECTED *Inquiry*

Refraction with Water GENERAL

👥 Small groups
🕐 10 minutes

LAB RATINGS

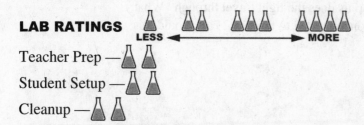

LESS ◄─────► MORE

Teacher Prep —
Student Setup —
Cleanup —

MATERIALS

For each group
• beaker (400 mL)
• pencil
• spoon
• ruler
• water

For each student
• goggles
• lab apron

SAFETY INFORMATION

Remind students to review all safety cautions and icons before beginning this lab. Remind students to pour water carefully and handle the beaker gently.

TEACHER NOTES

In this activity, students will explore light refraction by observing different objects through a beaker of water. Thicker objects (such as spoons or erasers) will be more noticeably magnified in the beaker of water. It is acceptable to substitute any classroom objects for the pencil and spoon, as long as they will not be damaged by the water.

Skills Focus Making Observations, Applying Concepts

My Notes

_____

_____

_____

_____

_____

MODIFICATION FOR INDEPENDENT *Inquiry*

Have students think about a time when they have noticed an object that is magnified by something else. (They may have noticed this with a magnifying glass, with curved mirrors, inside glasses of water, or at the pool.) Have students think about how they could explore the cause of this magnification. What materials could they use in the classroom? Have students brainstorm a list of materials and procedures. As they investigate, encourage students to think about how light bends, or *refracts,* as it travels from one material to another. How could this explain the magnification of the object?

Answer Key

2. Sample answer: The pencil looks thicker.
   Teacher Prompt Does the pencil look larger, smaller, or the same size when you look at it through the side of the beaker?
3. Answers will vary.
4. Sample answer: The spoon looks thicker.

Quick Lab continued

5. Answers will vary.

6. Sample answer: Each object looks larger when you look at it through the beaker of water.

7. Sample answer: The light bends when it travels from water to glass and then glass to air. This makes the object appear larger than it actually is.

   Teacher Prompt What different materials does the light travel through? What happens each time the light passes from one material to the next? How could this change the appearance of the image?

QUICK LAB DIRECTED *Inquiry*

Refraction with Water

In this lab, you will explore how light changes as it travels through different materials. You will observe how the size of a pencil and spoon appears to change when the objects are submerged in a beaker of water.

PROCEDURE

1 Fill the **beaker** about half-full with **water.**

2 Dip the top of the **pencil** into the beaker. Observe the pencil from the side of the beaker. Describe your observations.

_____

_____

_____

_____

_____

_____

3 Measure the thickness of the **spoon** using a **ruler.** Record your measurement.

_____

4 Dip the head of the spoon into the water, and observe the spoon from the side of the beaker. Describe your observations.

_____

_____

_____

_____

_____

_____

_____

OBJECTIVES

- Describe how light refracts through different materials.
- Describe how refracted light can distort the image of an object.

MATERIALS

For each group
- beaker (400 mL)
- pencil
- spoon
- ruler
- water

For each student
- goggles
- lab apron

Quick Lab continued

5 Hold a ruler up to the outside of the beaker, and measure the thickness of the spoon in the water. Record your measurement.

_____

6 How does the image of each object change when you look at it through the water in the beaker?

_____

_____

_____

_____

7 Recall that light refracts when it travels from one medium to another. How could this explain your observations of the objects in the water?

_____

_____

_____

_____

_____

_____

_____

_____

_____

_____

_____

_____

_____

EXPLORATION LAB DIRECTED Inquiry **AND** GUIDED Inquiry

Comparing Colors of Objects in Different Colors of Light GENERAL

👥 Small groups

🕐 45 minutes

LAB RATINGS

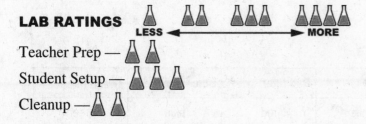

Teacher Prep —

Student Setup —

Cleanup —

MATERIALS

For each group
- acetate sheets, red, blue, green
- light source
- objects of different colors, white, black, red, yellow
- ruler, metric
- scissors
- shoe box with cover
- tape, masking

For each student
- safety goggles

SAFETY INFORMATION

Remind students to review all safety cautions and icons before beginning this lab. If students are using a lamp, warn them not to get their faces too close to the bulb when they are observing the objects in their light box.

TEACHER NOTES

In this activity, students will study the effect of different colors of light on objects of different colors. First, students will predict what color different objects will appear to be in each color of light. Next, students will build a light box to test their predictions. The acetate sheets are used as filters to project different colors of light on the different colored objects. The students will learn that the color of an object depends both on the wavelengths of the light that shines on it and the wavelengths that it reflects.

Tip This activity will help students explain what determines the color of certain objects. Premade filters of colored cellophane can also be used.

Student Tip Mixing light is not like mixing paint. When you combine blue and yellow paint, for instance, you end up with green paint. The same cannot be said for combining different colors of light.

Skills Focus Making Predictions, Evaluating Observations

My Notes

_____

_____

_____

_____

_____

MODIFICATION FOR INDEPENDENT Inquiry

Challenge students to develop their own procedures to test predictions of how objects of different colors appear in different colors of light.

Answer Key for DIRECTED Inquiry

ASK A QUESTION

1. Sample answer: An object appears a different color in colored light than it does in white light. You could investigate this by looking at different colored objects in different in colored lighting, and observing any color changes in the objects' colors.
   Teacher Prompt What are the two variables that you can consider when looking at an object?

FORM A PREDICTION

2. Sample table:

		No filter	Red filter	Blue filter	Green filter
Color of object	White	white	red	blue	green
	Black	black	red	blue	green
	Red	red	black	purple	brown
	Yellow	yellow	orange	green	black

3. Sample answer: I've noted that mixing paints is not the same as mixing lights. When you mix yellow and green paint, you get a light green paint. However, when yellow colored traffic lights shine on green objects, the objects seem black.
   Teacher Prompt What happens when you mix paints of different colors?

TEST THE PREDICTION

12. Students should get the following results:

		No filter	Red filter	Blue filter	Green filter
Color of object	White	white	red	blue	green
	Black	black	black	black	black
	Red	red	red	purple	yellow
	Yellow	yellow	orange	green	yellow-green

ANALYZE THE RESULTS

13. Sample answer: The results were consistent with the predictions in some cases but not in others.
    Teacher Prompt Which color-object combinations from your prediction table should you compare with the results table?

Exploration Lab continued

14. Sample answer: The results for the color filters, because my predictions for "no filter" were correct. Mixing red and green paint results in brown paint, but this is not so for light. Therefore, the way light mixes is different from the way paint mixes.
Teacher Prompt Is mixing paint the same as mixing light?

DRAW CONCLUSIONS

15. Sample answer: The color that an object reflects depends on the color of light shining on it. Reflected light is the color we see.
Teacher Prompt When you are looking at an object, what are you actually seeing?

Connect TO THE ESSENTIAL QUESTION

16. Sample answer: The color of an object depends both on the wavelengths of the light that shines on it and the wavelength(s) of light that it reflects.
Teacher Prompt What were the two basic variables you used in your light box experiment?

Answer Key for GUIDED Inquiry

ASK A QUESTION

1. Sample answer: An object appears a different color in colored light than it does in white light. You could investigate this by looking at different colored objects in different colored lighting and observing any change in the objects' colors.
Teacher Prompt What are two variables that you can consider when looking at an object?

FORM A PREDICTION

2. Some students may not consider observing the color of the objects under white light as necessary. Sample table:

		No filter	Red filter	Blue filter	Green filter
Color of object	White	white	red	blue	green
	Black	black	red	blue	green
	Red	red	black	purple	brown
	Yellow	yellow	orange	green	black

3. Sample answer: I've noted that mixing paints is not the same as mixing lights. When you mix yellow and green paint, you get a light green paint. However, when yellow colored traffic lights shine on green objects, the objects seem black.
Teacher Prompt What happens when you mix paints of different colors?

Exploration Lab continued

TEST THE PREDICTION

5. Sample answer: I could observe the color of the objects in the light box without a filter being in place (in white light).

7. Students should get the following results:

		No filter	Red filter	Blue filter	Green filter
Color of object	White	white	red	blue	green
	Black	black	black	black	black
	Red	red	red	purple	yellow
	Yellow	yellow	orange	green	yellow-green

ANALYZE THE RESULTS

8. Sample answer: The results are consistent with the predictions in some cases, but not in others.
Teacher Prompt Which color-object combinations from your prediction table should you compare with the results table?

9. Sample answer: Mixing red and green paint results in brown paint, but this is not so for light. Therefore, the way light mixes is different from the way paint mixes.
Teacher Prompt Is mixing paint the same as mixing light?

DRAW CONCLUSIONS

10. Sample answer: The color that an object reflects depends on the type of light shining on it. Reflected light is the color we see.
Teacher Prompt When you are looking at an object, what are you actually seeing?

Connect TO THE ESSENTIAL QUESTION

11. Sample answer: The color of an object depends both on the wavelengths of the light that shines on it and the wavelengths that it reflects. If certain wavelengths of light are absent from the incident light, these wavelengths are also absent from the reflected light.
Teacher Prompt What were the two basic variables you used in your light box experiment?

EXPLORATION LAB `DIRECTED Inquiry`

Comparing Colors of Objects in Different Colors of Light

In this lab, you will predict the effect of different colors of light on objects of different colors. Then you will build a light box to test your predictions.

PROCEDURE

ASK A QUESTION

❶ Have you been to a party or concert where the lighting was colored? How did the color of objects look different from how they normally look? How would you investigate why the color of objects appears different in colored lighting?

_____

_____

_____

FORM A PREDICTION

❷ In your experiment, you will shine light on different colored objects. You will have three different colored light filters and four different colored objects. Predict what color each object will appear to be in each color of light. Enter your predictions in the table below.

		No filter	Red filter	Blue filter	Green filter
Color of object	White				
	Black				
	Red				
	Yellow				

❸ Why did you make those predictions? Identify experiences you might have had to explain your predictions.

_____

_____

_____

OBJECTIVE
• Predict and determine the appearance of different colored objects in different colors of light.

MATERIALS
For each group
• acetate sheets, red, blue, green
• light source
• objects of different colors, white, black, red, yellow
• ruler, metric
• scissors
• shoe box with cover
• tape, masking
For each student
• safety goggles

Exploration Lab continued

TEST THE PREDICTION

4 Make three color filters. Use scissors to cut a 10 centimeter (cm) square from the sheet of red acetate. Do the same with the green and blue acetate.

5 To make the light box viewing hole, use scissors to cut a 3 cm hole at one end of the shoe box. You will view objects through this hole.

6 To make the light box filter hole, first use the ruler to measure a 6 cm square hole in the center of the cover of the shoe box. Use the scissors to cut the hole.

7 You will first observe the objects without the color filters. Place the light box on a flat surface near a strong white light source such as sunlight or a bright lamp. Position the box with the top facing the light source.

8 Place the white object in the center of the light box. Place the top on the light box.

9 Look through the viewing hole and observe the color of the object inside. Record your observation in the data table below.

10 To install the color filter, use masking tape to position the filters over the light hole. Apply the tape lightly since you will need to replace the filters several times

11 You will look at each of the four colored objects four times—once with no filter and once with red, blue, and green filters.

12 Use the light box to test each of the combinations of object color and filter. Record all of your observations in the table. Repeat this process using each of the three colored filters.

		No filter	Red filter	Blue filter	Green filter
Color of object	White				
	Black				
	Red				
	Yellow				

ANALYZE THE RESULTS

13 **Comparing Predictions** Compare your predictions (first table) to the results (second table). Are your results consistent with your predictions?

_____

_____

_____

Exploration Lab continued

⑭ Explaining Results Explain any differences between your results and your predictions.

_____

_____

_____

DRAW CONCLUSIONS

⑮ Making Inferences Why does the color of light cause the color of the objects to change?

_____

_____

_____

Connect TO THE ESSENTIAL QUESTION

⑯ Applying Concepts What determines an object's color?

_____

_____

_____

EXPLORATION LAB GUIDED *Inquiry*

Comparing Colors of Objects in Different Colors of Light

In this lab, you will predict the effect of different colors of light on objects of different colors. Then you will build a light box to test your predictions.

PROCEDURE

ASK A QUESTION

1 Have you been to a party or concert where the lighting was colored? How did the color of objects look different from normal? How would you investigate why the color of objects appears different in colored lighting?

_____

_____

_____

FORM A PREDICTION

2 In your experiment, you will shine light on different colored objects. You will have three different colored light filters and four different colored objects. Predict what color each object will appear to be in each color of light, and create a table below for your predictions.

OBJECTIVE
- Predict and determine the appearance of different colored objects in different colors of light.

MATERIALS
For each group
- acetate sheets, red, blue, green
- light source
- objects of different colors, white, black, red, yellow
- ruler, metric
- scissors
- shoe box with cover
- tape, masking

For each student
- safety goggles

Exploration Lab continued

3 Why did you make those predictions? Use various experiences you might have had to explain your predictions.

_____

_____

_____

TEST THE PREDICTION

4 Use the three colors of acetate to make light filters.

5 Make a light box with the shoe box. Make a small hole to view objects and a larger hole for the light filter. What would you do to create a control in this investigation?

6 Install the color filter, and carry out your tests. Be sure to use a strong white light source such as sunlight or a bright lamp. Position the box with the top facing the light source.

7 Create another table to record your observations.

ANALYZE THE RESULTS

8 **Comparing Predictions** Compare your predictions (first table) to the results (second table). Are your results consistent with your predictions?

_____

_____

_____

9 **Explaining Results** Explain any differences between your results and your predictions.

_____

_____

_____

Exploration Lab continued

DRAW CONCLUSIONS

10 **Making Inferences** Why does the color of light cause the color of the object to change?

_____

_____

_____

Connect TO THE ESSENTIAL QUESTION

11 **Applying Concepts** What determines an object's color?

_____

_____

_____

QUICK LAB GUIDED *Inquiry*

Spoon Images GENERAL

👥 Student pairs

🕐 15 minutes

LAB RATINGS

LESS ◄————————► MORE

Teacher Prep —

Student Setup —

Cleanup —

MATERIALS

For each group

- diffuse reflective object (wooden block, cardboard, paper, etc.)
- mirror, flat
- spoon, metal

TEACHER NOTES

In this activity, students will work with a partner to examine the images reflected by a diffuse reflective object, a flat mirror, concave mirror (inside of spoon), and a convex mirror (outside of a spoon). Students will also begin to use a simple ray diagram as a model to explain the reflection of light from the different surfaces.

Tip Clean, shiny spoons make the best reflective surfaces. You may need to draw examples of ray diagrams for students to refer to.

Skills Focus Making Observations, Making Inferences

My Notes

_____

_____

_____

_____

_____

MODIFICATION FOR INDEPENDENT *Inquiry*

Tell students that you want them to investigate how images are formed by different types of mirrors, using only a small flat mirror and a shiny spoon. Have students write a quick procedure using these materials. Challenge students to explain their observations using words and pictures.

MODIFICATION FOR DIRECTED *Inquiry*

Ask students "How do flat and curved mirrors form images?" Use the Guided Inquiry questions but supplement them with specific questions to consider for each surface.

Quick Lab continued

Answer Key

1. Accept all reasonable answers.

2. Accept all reasonable answers. Image should appear upside down.

3. Accept all reasonable answers. Image should appear right side up.

4. No. Accept all reasonable answers that include the idea that light is scattered or diffused when it reflects off of rough surfaces. Students should understand that light is reflected from the paper even though it is not a shiny surface that produces a reflected image.

5. Diagrams of the mirrored surfaces should show the light ray reflecting in a predictable way (angle of incidence). Diagrams of the rough surface should show the light reflecting in different directions.

QUICK LAB GUIDED *Inquiry*

Spoon Images

In this lab, you will compare the images you detect when observing a flat mirror, a concave mirror, and a convex mirror. You will then explain how light reflects from the three different surfaces to form the images we see.

PROCEDURE

1 With your partner, observe the virtual image of your face in the flat mirror. Describe the image below. Note the size, clarity, and orientation (right side up/upside down) of the image.

_____

_____

2 Using the inside of the spoon as a concave mirror, observe the image of your face in the curved mirror. Describe the image below. Note the size, clarity, and orientation (right side up /upside down) of the image.

_____

_____

3 Now, use the back of the spoon as a convex mirror and observe the image of your face in the curved mirror. Describe the image below. Note the size, clarity, and orientation (right side up/upside down) of the image.

_____

_____

4 Pick an object such as the back of your paper that does not have a shiny surface. Look at the object and note any observations of reflection. Do you see a reflected image? Explain why or why not.

_____

_____

_____

_____

OBJECTIVES

- Describe the way that lenses and mirrors form images.
- Describe how some objects reflect light in many different directions, while other objects reflect light in a uniform way.

MATERIALS

- diffuse reflective object (wooden block, cardboard, paper, etc.)
- mirror, flat
- spoon, metal

Quick Lab continued

5 Your teacher will show you a single ray diagram of light as an arrow. Imagine that the arrow represents the light reflecting from your face to the mirror. Draw a light ray diagram that shows how the light is reflecting from each of the surfaces.

_____

_____

_____

_____

_____

QUICK LAB DIRECTED Inquiry

Mirror Images GENERAL

👥 Student pairs
🕐 20 minutes

LAB RATINGS

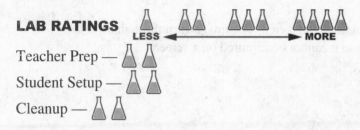

LESS ←——————————→ MORE

Teacher Prep —
Student Setup —
Cleanup —

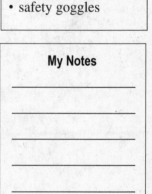

MATERIALS
For each group
• candle (or battery-operated candle)
• card, index
• jar lid
• matches
• mirror, concave
• mirror, convex (optional)
For each student
• safety goggles

SAFETY INFORMATION

Remind students to review all safety cautions and icons before beginning this lab. If using a real candle in this lab, remind students of safety precautions when using an open flame.

TEACHER NOTES

In this activity, students will use a flat mirror to find a virtual image and a concave mirror to find a real image. Remember that the image we see in a flat mirror is called a virtual image. A virtual image is an image from which light appears to diverge. Rays do not pass through a virtual image, so a screen at the image location doesn't show the image. A concave mirror, on the other hand, forms a real image where light from the object converges and actually passes through the image. You can put a screen at that location and see the image. We will be using an index card as a screen to capture the reflected, real image of the candle flame. Make clear to the students the difference between real and virtual images, and how to capture a real image on a screen.

My Notes
_____
_____
_____
_____
_____

Tip As an alternative to a traditional candle, you may want to use a battery-operated candle.

Student Tip You will need to move the index card in order to capture the image of the candle.

Skills Focus Making Observations, Making Predictions

MODIFICATION FOR GUIDED Inquiry

Ask the students, "How are the images formed by a flat mirror different from the images formed by a concave mirror?" Have the students use the same materials as in the directed lab, but ask them to come up with their own procedure for making and recording observations with the concave mirror.

Answer Key

1. Accept all reasonable answers.

2. Behind the mirror. Same size as the object. Right-side up.

4. The image was in front of the concave mirror. The image appeared to be smaller. The image was upside-down.

5. Accept all reasonable answers. Sample answer: I disagree. The image seen through a magnifying glass is a virtual image because it cannot be captured on a screen.

QUICK LAB **DIRECTED** *Inquiry*

Mirror Images

In this lab, you will investigate the different types of images formed by a flat mirror compared to the images formed by a concave mirror (shaped like the inside of a spoon).

PROCEDURE

❶ Your teacher just demonstrated a virtual image using a large flat mirror. What did you notice about the virtual image?

_____

❷ Use a small flat mirror to examine your own virtual image and to help answer the following questions: Where was the image? What was the size of the image? Was the image right side up or upside down?

_____

❸ Now you will observe a real image using a different kind of mirror known as a concave mirror. Observe how your teacher has arranged the concave mirror, candle, and index card. Move your index card slowly toward and away from the candle until you can see the real image of the candle on the card.

❹ What do you notice about the real image of the candle? Where is the image? What is the size of the image? Is the image right side up or upside down?

_____

_____

❺ A student claims, "I think the image I see through a magnifying glass is a real image." Do you agree or disagree? Explain your thinking.

_____

_____

_____

OBJECTIVE

• Investigate real and virtual images.

MATERIALS

For each group
• candle
• card, index
• jar lid
• matches
• mirror, concave
For each student
• safety goggles

Light Maze ADVANCED

👥 Student pairs
🕐 45 minutes

LAB RATINGS

LESS ⟷ MORE

Teacher Prep —
Student Setup —
Cleanup —

MATERIALS

For each group
• box, shoe
• flashlight
• mirrors, small, flat
• protractor
• scissors
• tagboard/cardboard
• tape, masking

For each student
• safety goggles

SAFETY INFORMATION

Remind students to review all safety cautions and icons before beginning this lab. Use caution when cutting boxes and handling mirrors, as some edges can be sharp.

TEACHER NOTES

In this lab, students will investigate the variables that affect the success of a series of mirrors to reflect light through a "light maze." Students will use the design process to solve the design challenge to build a light maze that directs light around at least three 90 degree angles. Students will be given constraints on the materials they may use to solve the challenge. Small balls of clay work well to hold mirrors in place. Warn students that the light may be very bright when they look into the mirrors. You may cut the holes yourself prior to class using a sharp knife.

Tip Students may need a reminder to take time to plan before building. You may also want to use a more powerful light source such as a projector (or a laser pointer) if the flashlights are not providing the needed results.

Student Tip Think about what you already know about light and reflection.

Skills Focus Solving a Problem, Making a Plan, Testing a Solution

MODIFICATION FOR DIRECTED Inquiry

Provide a working model of a light maze (with the top removed so that students can observe the positions of the mirrors) and allow students to refer to the model as they work through the procedure on the Student Datasheet. To make this lab even more directed, you can give students specific step-by-step directions for building a light maze.

My Notes

_____
_____
_____
_____
_____

S.T.E.M. Lab continued

Answer Key for GUIDED Inquiry

ASK A QUESTION

2. Accept all reasonable answers. If not mentioned, note the angle of the mirrors.

DEVELOP A PLAN

3. Accept all reasonable answers. Provide guidance as necessary on plans.

TEST THE PROTOTYPE

8. Accept all reasonable answers.

EVALUATE THE PROTOTYPE

9. Accept all reasonable answers.

DRAW CONCLUSIONS

10. See light, the flashlight, my partner, etc. This is a virtual image.

11. The angle of the mirrors was important so that the light can reflect from one mirror to another.

Connect TO THE ESSENTIAL QUESTION

12. Disagree. Reasons may vary but should include a reference to the mirror being more reflective than the inside of the box.

Answer Key for INDEPENDENT Inquiry

ASK A QUESTION

2. Accept all reasonable answer. If not mentioned, note the angle of the mirrors.

DEVELOP A PLAN

3. Accept all reasonable answers. Provide guidance as necessary on plans.

TEST THE PROTOTYPE

8. Accept all reasonable answers.

9. Accept all reasonable answers.

EVALUATE THE PROTOTYPE

10. Accept all reasonable answers.

S.T.E.M. Lab continued

DRAW CONCLUSIONS

11. Students should note that this is a virtual image.

12. Accept any that note that the angle of the mirrors was important because the light needed to reflect from one mirror to another.

Connect TO THE ESSENTIAL QUESTION

13. Disagree. Reasons may vary but should include a reference to the mirror being more reflective than the inside of the box.

S.T.E.M. LAB GUIDED Inquiry

Light Maze

In this lab, you will use your understanding of light, mirrors, and reflection to solve a design challenge. You are challenged to design, build, and test a light maze. Light should enter your light maze through one opening, reflect around several corners, and finally exit through a second opening. Your maze must meet the following criteria:

- The maze must contain one opening for light to enter and one opening for light to exit.
- Light entering must make at least three "turns" before exiting the maze.
- The maze may only be constructed using materials listed.

PROCEDURE

MAKE OBSERVATIONS

1 On the top of your table, position a flashlight and two mirrors so that light reflects from one mirror to the other mirror, to your partner's eye.

ASK A QUESTION

2 What do you notice about the positions of the mirrors? What do you notice about the angle of the mirrors?

_____

_____

OBJECTIVES
- Apply the law of reflection while solving a problem.
- Describe the ways in which lenses and mirrors form images.

MATERIALS
For each group
- box, shoe
- flashlight
- mirrors, small, flat
- protractor
- scissors
- tagboard/cardboard
- tape, masking
For each student
- safety goggles

S.T.E.M. Lab continued

DEVELOP A PLAN

3 Using what you noticed about the position of the mirrors in Step 1, quickly sketch a labeled diagram for a light maze in the space below. Note the position of the mirrors and the locations of the opening and exit. Ask your teacher to check your plan before moving to Step 4.

BUILD A PROTOTYPE

4 Open the shoe box. Poke starter holes with pencils and then carefully cut the holes out with scissors to allow light to enter and exit the maze. Label these openings "entrance" and "exit."

5 Position the mirrors as shown in your plan. Use masking tape and cardboard to position the mirrors correctly.

6 Put the lid on the light maze.

TEST THE PROTOTYPE

7 Test the prototype by shining the flashlight into the entrance.

8 Record your observations of the light at the exit. Was your prototype successful in meeting the challenge?

_____

EVALUATE THE PROTOTYPE

9 Analyze the prototype light maze you constructed. Did you encounter any problems while meeting the challenge? If so, describe how you would modify your light maze to eliminate those problems.

_____

_____

S.T.E.M. Lab continued

DRAW CONCLUSIONS

⑩ **Applying Concepts** When you look through the exit hole into the light maze, what do you see? Is this image a real or virtual image?

_____

_____

⑪ **Explaining Methods** Explain why the angle of the mirrors in the light maze was important for solving the challenge.

_____

_____

_____

Connect **TO THE ESSENTIAL QUESTION**

⑫ **Applying Concepts** A student says, "I don't think we need the mirrors. The light will shine out of the exit just as brightly without mirrors." Do you agree or disagree? Explain your thinking.

_____

_____

_____

S.T.E.M. LAB INDEPENDENT *Inquiry*

Light Maze

In this lab, you will use your understanding of light, mirrors, and reflection to solve a design challenge. You are challenged to design, build, and test a light maze. Light should enter your light maze through one opening, reflect around several corners, and finally exit through a second opening. Your maze must meet the following criteria:

- The maze must contain one opening for light to enter and one opening for light to exit.
- Light entering must make at least three "turns" before exiting the maze.
- The maze must be constructed using only the materials provided.

PROCEDURE

MAKE OBSERVATIONS

❶ On the top of your table, position a flashlight and two mirrors so that light reflects from one mirror to the other mirror, to your partner's eye.

ASK A QUESTION

❷ What do you notice about the positions of the mirrors?

_____

_____

_____

_____

OBJECTIVES

- Apply the law of reflection while solving a problem.
- Describe the ways in which lenses and mirrors form images.

MATERIALS

For each group
- box, shoe
- flashlight
- mirrors, small, flat
- protractor
- scissors
- tagboard/cardboard
- tape, masking

For each student
- safety goggles

S.T.E.M. Lab continued

DEVELOP A PLAN

3 Using what you noticed about the position of the mirrors in Step 1, quickly sketch a labeled diagram for a light maze in the space below. Note the position of the mirrors and the locations of the opening and exit. Ask your teacher to check your plan before moving to Step 4.

BUILD A PROTOTYPE

4 Carefully prepare your container by removing one side (this will later become the top). If you picked a shoe box, simply open the top.

5 Poke starter holes with pencils and then carefully cut the holes out to allow light to enter and exit the maze. Label these openings "entrance" and "exit".

6 Position the mirrors as shown in your plan. Use masking tape and cardboard to position the mirrors correctly.

7 Put the lid on the light maze.

TEST THE PROTOTYPE

8 How will you check that your mirrors are positioned correctly?

_____

_____

S.T.E.M. Lab continued

9 Test your light maze and record your observations below.

_____

_____

EVALUATE THE PROTOTYPE

10 Analyze the prototype light maze you constructed. Did you encounter any problems while meeting the challenge? If so, describe how you would modify your light maze to eliminate those problems.

_____

_____

_____

DRAW CONCLUSIONS

11 **Applying Concepts** When you look through the exit hole into the light maze, what do you see? Is this image a real or virtual image?

_____

_____

12 **Explaining Methods** Explain why the angle of the mirrors in the light maze was important for solving the challenge.

_____

_____

Connect TO THE ESSENTIAL QUESTION

13 **Applying Concepts** A student says, "I don't think we need the mirrors. The light will shine out of the exit just as brightly without mirrors." Do you agree or disagree? Explain your thinking.

_____

_____

_____

QUICK LAB GUIDED Inquiry

Shapes and Sight BASIC

👥 Small groups
🕐 20 minutes

LAB RATINGS

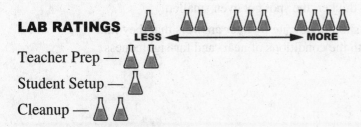

LESS ← → MORE

Teacher Prep —

Student Setup —

Cleanup —

MATERIALS

For each group
• flashlight
• paper
• pen or pencil
• plastic bag, sealable, sandwich size
• water

For each student
• safety goggles

SAFETY INFORMATION

Remind students to review all safety cautions and icons before beginning this lab. Keep paper towels on hand to clean up any spills. Spilled water should be mopped up immediately to avoid slippery floors. Upon completion of the inquiry, be sure that students empty the water from their plastic bags or balloons into a sink.

TEACHER NOTES

In this activity, students explore how the shape of a lens affects its focus. They will first observe the pattern the flashlight creates on a piece of paper, then using a sealable plastic bag filled with water as a model of the lens of an eye. If sealable plastic bags are not available, balloons may be used instead. Students will work in teams to evaluate the effect that the shape of the lens has on the pattern created by the flashlight.

Alternatively, the students could tape the paper to a wall, hang the bag from one hand, and shine the light through it with the other hand.

Tip While students are working through the lab, encourage them to pay attention to details such as the angle of the flashlight, the distance between it and the "lens," and the medium used within the lens. How many factors can they identify as subjects for further investigation?

Student Tip What happens to light when it moves through a medium other than air?

Skills Focus Making Predictions, Creating Drawings

MODIFICATION FOR GUIDED Inquiry

Start by having the students examine drawings of the shape of the eye relative to nearsightedness and farsightedness then have them start their own inquiry by filling a sealable plastic bag with water and observing how the bag changes the shape of a spot of light from a flashlight. Encourage them to use what they learned from the diagram to design their own investigation with their model of a lens.

My Notes

_____

_____

_____

_____

_____

Answer Key

3. Accept all reasonable answers.

4. Sample answer: The spot of light got smaller as the flashlight moved toward the paper.

5. Sample answer: The bright spot at the center got smaller.

6. Sample answer: When we made the lens thicker, the spot got even smaller.

7. Accept all reasonable answers. Students should indicate by their answers that they link the shape of the water lens or eyeball with the conditions of near- and far-sightedness.

QUICK LAB GUIDED *Inquiry*

Shapes and Sight

In this lab, you will see what happens to a spot of light when you shine a flashlight through a plastic bag filled with water.

PROCEDURE

1 Place a piece of paper on the table.

2 Hold the flashlight about a foot above the table, shining its light at the paper. Trace the circle of light on the paper with a pen or pencil.

3 Predict what you think will happen as you move the flashlight toward the paper.

_____

_____

4 Move the light about six inches toward the paper. What happens to the spot of light?

_____

_____

5 Fill a plastic bag with water to model a lens. Make sure there is no air bubble in the bag. Have one person hold the lens above the paper while another person holds the flashlight above the lens. What happens to the circle of light on the paper now? Trace this new circle on the paper and label it.

_____

_____

OBJECTIVES

- Use a model for a lens to observe how it affects light.
- Compare the model to the lens in a human eye.

MATERIALS

For each group
- flashlight
- paper
- pen or pencil
- plastic bag, sealable, sandwich size
- water

For each student
- safety goggles

Quick Lab continued

6 Have the person holding the lens push both their hands together to compress the lens. Does the spot of light appear the same as it did before? Trace and label the circle as before.

_____

_____

7 Relate what you observed to vision. How does this lab relate to nearsightedness and farsightedness?

_____

_____

_____

QUICK LAB GUIDED Inquiry

Investigating Vision BASIC

👥 Small groups

🕐 20 minutes

LAB RATINGS

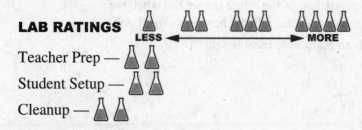

LESS ← → MORE

Teacher Prep —

Student Setup —

Cleanup —

MATERIALS

For each group
- convex lens
- Fresnel lens (or larger convex lens)
- lamp
- paper plate, white
- ruler, metric

For each student
- safety goggles

SAFETY INFORMATION

Remind students to review all safety cautions and icons before beginning this lab. Caution students that light bulbs get very hot and can cause burns. Be sure they turn the lamp on only for the time periods needed to collect data.

My Notes

_____

_____

_____

_____

_____

TEACHER NOTES

In this activity, students learn how distance affects vision and how the parts of the eye work together to create an image. They will set up a lamp, a convex lens, and a paper plate to observe how far the plate has to be from the lens to allow light from the lamp to be in focus on the plate. Students can then change the lamp and lens locations and repeat the test. They will then introduce an additional lens and observe its effect on the setup.

Tip While students are working through the lab, have them think about what parts of the eye correspond to the materials used in this lab and what roles those parts play in vision.

Student Tip What is one of the key characteristics of lenses?

Skills Focus Collecting Data, Constructing Tables, Evaluating Models

MODIFICATION FOR INDEPENDENT Inquiry

Have students identify the key components of the eye, then give them the materials and have them figure out which item corresponds to which part of the eye. Assign them the task of investigating how distance affects vision and allow them to develop and execute a procedure to investigate that task.

Answer Key

3. Sample answer: The distance between the plate and lens gets smaller.

5. Sample answer: The additional lens decreased the distance we had to move the plate to focus the image.

6. Sample answer: No. Instead of moving the position of the retina (as we did when we moved the plate), the eye changes the shape of the lens, which changes its focal point.

7. Sample answer: We could use a lens with an adjustable focal length.

QUICK LAB GUIDED Inquiry

Investigating Vision

In this lab, you will investigate vision and determine how different parts of the eye work together to make vision possible.

PROCEDURE

1 Arrange the materials so that light from the lamp is directed through the convex lens onto the plate which is sitting on the table/desk. The lens should be about 2/3 meter (70 cm) from the lamp.

2 Move the plate to adjust the distance between the plate and the lens by moving the lens until you see a focused image of the bulb on the plate. Measure this distance and record it in a data table that you construct below.

3 Place the plate on the floor under the light. Move the lens until it is about 1.5 m from the lamp. Adjust the lens once again to get a focused image, then measure the distance between the plate and the lens. How does the distance between the plate and the lens change when the lens is farther from the lamp?

_____

_____

_____

OBJECTIVES

- Explain how the cornea, lens, and retina work together to focus and detect light.

MATERIALS

For each group
- convex lens
- Fresnel lens (or larger convex lens)
- lamp
- paper plate, white
- ruler, metric

For each student
- safety goggles

Quick Lab continued

4 Repeat Steps 1 through 3 adding the second lens (Fresnel or larger convex lens) to the set-up. Measure this distance and record it in a data table that you construct below.

5 How does the addition of the second lens affect your results?

_____

_____

_____

6 Your eye uses a lens to focus an image. When the eye focuses an image, does it use the same procedure you used in this activity? Explain.

_____

_____

_____

7 How could you change the set-up to make it model the way that the eye focuses an image?

_____

_____

_____

QUICK LAB INDEPENDENT Inquiry

Light Technology in Color Monitors GENERAL

👥 Small groups
🕐 15 minutes

LAB RATINGS

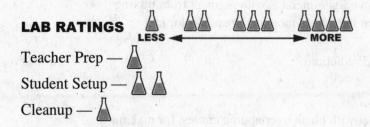

LESS ⟵⟶ MORE

Teacher Prep —

Student Setup —

Cleanup —

MATERIALS

For the class
• color television and/or computer monitor

For each group
• flashlights (3)
• magnifying glass
• markers, permanent (1 red, 1 green, 1 blue)
• paper, white
• rubber bands (3)
• wrap, plastic

For each student
• safety goggles

SAFETY INFORMATION

Remind students to review all safety cautions and icons before beginning this lab.

TEACHER NOTES

In this activity, students will explore how computer and television monitors create images that include white, black, and millions of colors using only three colors of additive light. First, students will use a magnifying glass to observe the groups of red/blue/green pixels on a TV or computer screen. Then, the students will use permanent markers to make red, green, and blue filters on small pieces of plastic food wrap. They will place the filters over the flashlight lens and hold them in place with rubber bands. In the darkened classroom, students will then shine the flashlights onto white paper, allowing the colors to overlap. Students will predict what will happen if they put all three filters onto one flashlight — will they get white light or no light? Then they test the prediction. (The correct answer is almost no light; it is nearly all absorbed by the three filtering layers.)

For best results, choose identical flashlights that make a large, even, central "spot" of white light. LED flashlights work well. Red is the strongest color and can be overpowering. To help with this, have the student holding the red light back up to reduce the intensity. Provide strong magnifying glasses and/or low-resolution screens so that students can easily observe the pixels.

Through advance homework, an introductory lesson, or as guidance during the activity, provide students with the following background information on the color theory of light: *Subtractive color* starts with white light, which contains all colors (as can be demonstrated with a prism). When the light strikes the pigment in paint, the pigment absorbs or "subtracts" some frequencies and reflects others. We perceive those reflections as the color of the paint. The color is not "in the paint" but in the incident light. When all of the pigments are combined, black paint results because all of the frequencies of light have been absorbed.

My Notes

_____

_____

_____

_____

_____

Quick Lab continued

By contrast, *additive color* starts with black, or the absence of light. Green and blue light combine to make cyan, red and blue make magenta, and red and green make yellow. All together they "add up to" white light. An electronic display is made of thousands of tiny groups of light-emitting red, green, and blue colored stripes or dots called "pixels" (short for "picture elements"). Because the colored pixels are so close together, our eyes interpret the combinations as either white or a specific color. Eliminating the pixel light creates a black area such as you see when your computer monitor is turned off.

Tip Students may already be familiar with how light interacts with pigment from mixing paints in art class. Ensure they understand that light from monitors creates color in a different way.

Skills Focus Making Observations, Making Predictions

MODIFICATION FOR GUIDED *Inquiry*

Provide support, such as a data table or a sheet with blank overlapping circles, for making and recording the observations of different combinations of light from the flashlights.

Answer Key

1. There are tiny groups of red, blue, and green stripes or dots.

5. Predictions will vary. Sample answers: We will see white light. OR We will see no light.

6. Sample answer: We saw almost no light.

7. All of the light frequencies were absorbed by one of the filters.
   Teacher Prompt How do the filters work to create colored light?

QUICK LAB INDEPENDENT *Inquiry*

Light Technology in Color Monitors

Visual displays of information are a large part of how people interact with technology. Electronic devices such as televisions, computers, and mobile phones have lighted screens that display a range of colors. In this activity, you will explore how these devices produce colors.

PROCEDURE

1 Turn on the television or monitor and set the display to a multicolored scene. Take turns with your classmates using the magnifying glass to examine the lit screen closely. What do you observe?

_____

_____

2 Use the permanent markers and the plastic food wrap to make colored light filters. Color an area on each sheet that will cover the flashlight lens completely.

3 Place the filters on the flashlights and secure them in place with the rubber bands.

4 In a darkened classroom, shine the flashlights onto the white paper in different combinations. Make a table on a separate sheet of paper to record your observations of each combination you try.

5 If the colored filters were all placed on one flashlight, what color would result? Record your prediction here.

_____

_____

6 Put all the filters on one flashlight and test your prediction. What result do you see?

_____

_____

7 Why did you get the result you observed in Step 6?

_____

_____

OBJECTIVES

- Closely examine light-producing screens.
- Use colored light to explore additive light.

MATERIALS

For the class
- color television and/or computer monitor

For each group
- flashlights (3)
- magnifying glass
- markers, permanent (1 red, 1 green, 1 blue)
- paper, white
- rubber bands (3)
- wrap, plastic

For each student
- lab apron
- safety goggles

QUICK LAB DIRECTED *Inquiry*

Total Internal Reflection GENERAL

👥 Small groups
🕐 20 minutes

LAB RATINGS

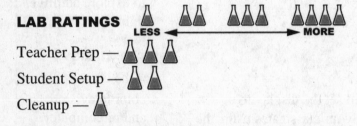

LESS ◄————————► MORE

Teacher Prep —

Student Setup —

Cleanup —

SAFETY INFORMATION

Remind students to review all safety cautions and icons before beginning this lab. Instruct students in the appropriate use of the laser pointers that will be used in this lab. Students should never shine the laser beam in their own or others' eyes. Remind students to be careful when moving around the darkened classroom.

TEACHER NOTES

In this activity, students will work in small groups to observe total internal reflection of a laser beam in a stream of water. Before beginning the activity, explain that transparent materials, such as air, water, and glass, refract light when it travels from one medium to another. Under certain conditions, if a beam of light travels from one medium toward another at a glancing angle, it will not refract into the second medium, but reflect off of the interface and continue on its way in the first. To demonstrate this effect, place a clear, flat-sided container of water near the edge of a table and a small object on the other side. From a position below the table edge, students will be able to see the reflection of the object on the underside of the water's surface but not the object directly.

MATERIALS

For each group
- beaker or tumbler, clear plastic
- bottle, clear plastic, 2 L, prepared
- laser pointer, red, <5mW, class II or IIIa
- sink or tub
- water

For each student
- lab apron

My Notes

_____

_____

_____

_____

_____

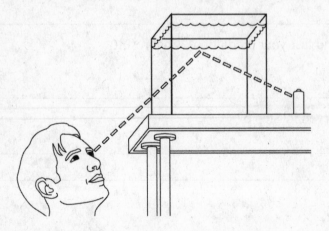

Quick Lab continued

Further explain that this effect is used in optical fibers. Pulses of laser light travel in glass fibers, which have a core of high-refractive-index glass. The light travels in a straight line until it reaches a bend in the fiber. If the turn is not too sharp, the light reflects down the core instead of escaping out the sides of the fiber.

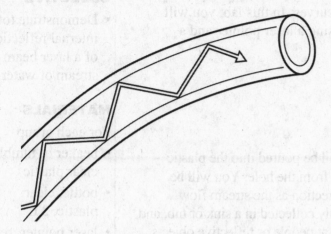

The students will be able to observe this effect as they carry out the procedure for the quick lab in a darkened classroom. They shine a laser pointer beam through a water-filled clear plastic bottle with a small hole in the side. As the water streams out into a sink or tub, the beam will remain in the stream as it curves down, and will be invisible until the water flow becomes turbulent. For a nice effect, students can catch the water in the beaker just as it does.

Prior to the lab, prepare one container for each group. Poke a small hole with a nail about 4 mm in diameter about 5 cm from the bottom of a 2-liter plastic soda bottle. It is important that the stream of water be laminar at first, so use a small round file to make the sides of the hole smooth. If necessary, saw off the top of the container so that you can sand the inside surface. The students will probably want to refill the containers several times.

Tip Laser light is pulsed as it travels down the fiber, transmitting information.

Skills Focus Making Observations, Applying Concepts

MODIFICATION FOR GUIDED Inquiry

Provide students with the same materials and direction on the safe use of the lasers, including keeping them dry. Explain the principles of optical fiber. Instruct them to find a way to use the materials to demonstrate total internal reflection.

Answer Key

3. Sample answer: The beam goes through the container and is reflected a little around the edges of the hole. It travels in the water as long as the flow is smooth, even when the water bends downward. When the flow breaks up, the light escapes and can be seen.

4. Sample answer: The angles of the light beams change. You can see it bouncing off the walls of the water fiber in different ways.

QUICK LAB DIRECTED Inquiry

Total Internal Reflection

An important application of lasers is data transmission through optical fibers. Laser light normally travels in a straight line; with optical fibers, it can be made to travel around curves. In this lab, you will demonstrate how optical fiber works using a laser pointer and a curving "fiber" of water.

PROCEDURE

1 Arrange your work area. Water will be poured into the plastic container and will exit as a stream from the hole. You will be directing laser light in the same direction as the stream flow. Ensure that the stream will be neatly collected in a sink or tub, and that laser light will not be directed at people or reflective objects.

2 Fill the container with water. Allow a small stream of water — the "fiber" — to come out of the hole and fall into the sink or tub.

3 From the opposite side of the container, direct the laser pointer light to shine through the container and enter the water stream. Record your observations.

_____

_____

_____

OBJECTIVE

• Demonstrate total internal reflection of a laser beam in a stream of water.

MATERIALS

For each group

• beaker or tumbler, clear plastic

• bottle, clear plastic, 2 L

• laser pointer, red, <5mW, class II or IIIa

• sink or tub

• water

For each student

• lab apron

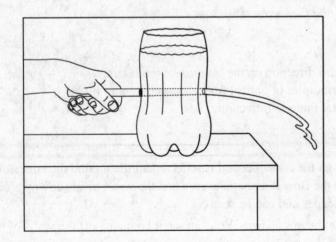

Quick Lab continued

④ View the setup from above and move the pointer back and forth slightly.
Record your observations.

_____

_____

⑤ For an interesting effect, use the beaker or tumbler to "catch" the light in the
stream of water.

EXPLORATION LAB GUIDED Inquiry **AND** INDEPENDENT Inquiry

Investigating Artificial Light GENERAL

🪑 Small groups

🕐 45 minutes

LAB RATINGS

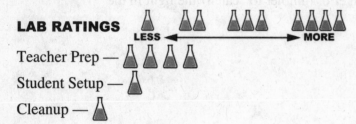

LESS ◄————————► MORE

Teacher Prep —

Student Setup —

Cleanup —

SAFETY INFORMATION

Remind students to review all safety cautions and icons before beginning this lab. Caution students to be careful when measuring air temperature near hot bulbs and when handling delicate glass bulbs. Point out the locations of any extension cords on the floor and tape them down.

TEACHER NOTES

In this activity, students will quantitatively and qualitatively compare artificial lighting types. To prepare for the lab, guide students in collecting or provide background information about light bulbs. Topics to cover include:

- bulb types for residential use
- disposal and safety issues
- wattage and energy use
- lumens
- running temperature
- color temperature
- use life
- whether they are dimmable
- best applications

MATERIALS

For each station
- binders, empty (2)
- lamp
- light bulb, approx. 800 lumens
- light bulb color temperature graphic (optional)
- objects, small, colored (1 set)
- ruler, metric
- textbook
- thermometer

For each student
- safety goggles

My Notes

_____

_____

_____

_____

_____

In the Guided Inquiry, small groups of students will circulate around several different lighting stations set up on a table or circle of desks. At each station, set up a lamp with a shade and a lit bulb that is rated to give off approximately 800 lumens. Have the lamps lit before and throughout the activity so that they maintain a constant running temperature. As resources permit, provide a second unlit bulb for examination. To keep an unlit bulb from rolling off the table, place it on a folded towel in a shallow dish. Set empty binders up on their edges to separate stations' light while allowing side-by-side comparisons. Place an identical set of colored objects and textbooks open to the same page with a photographic spread under each lamp. Finally, provide the bulb packaging, or label each station with the name of the bulb, its cost, and its expected life in hours.

Exploration Lab continued

In the Independent Inquiry, provide the class with the same materials as for the Guided Inquiry, but not set up in any particular way. Depending on the number of lamps and bulbs available, direct small groups or the entire class to develop a plan for comparing the bulbs and their light with one another and allow them to execute the plan with your approval.

Examples of bulb types and ratings that give off approximately 800 lumens:

- 60W incandescent
- 14W compact fluorescent (CFL)
- 12W LED
- 60W halogen

Examples of color temperature names and approximate color temperatures:

- "soft white" or "warm white" (2700 K) – orange-yellow light
- "bright white" (3000 K) – light yellow light
- "cool white" (4100 K) – white light with a tinge of blue
- "daylight" (5000 K) – blue-white light
- "super daylight" (6400 K) – blue-white light, as with an overcast sky

Note that in color temperature, blue occurs at higher color temperatures, while red occurs at lower color temperatures. This is the opposite of what you might expect in that as red is typically thought of as hot, and blue is thought of as cold.

Examples of colored objects for best comparison:

- white clothing item, such as a cotton sock
- strong red, green (especially plants), and blue items
- skin tones, such as one hand held under each lamp

A standard color chart showing light bulb color temperatures is often shown on bulb packaging. Another source for this information is www. eere.energy.gov; go to this site and search the key words: "color temperature."

Tip Consumer interest in alternatives and energy legislation will result in fewer incandescent bulbs in residential use. Students can use information in this lab to make informed choices about artificial lighting technology.

Skills Focus Making Observations

MODIFICATION FOR DIRECTED (Inquiry)

Set up the activity as for the Guided Inquiry. Provide students with a structured worksheet and/or data table to fill out as they make their observations.

Answer Key for GUIDED (Inquiry)

MAKE OBSERVATIONS

4. Sample answer: The LED bulb is shaped like a regular light bulb but is opaque and seems sturdier than glass. It is gray and bright yellow and looks like it has cooling fins on it. It looks more like some kind of a doorknob than a light bulb.

5. Sample answer: The air 5 cm next to the LED bulb is 22 °C, only 1° warmer than the room.

6. Sample answer: The color of the LED bulb's light is like the incandescent bulb, kind of orange and yellow, but a little less orange and a little more white. According to the color chart, it is 2700 K.

7. Sample answer: The LED light seems comfortable and warm, not too bright.

8. Sample answer: The wattage of the LED bulb is 12 watts.

9. Sample answer: The objects looked almost the same compared to the ones under the incandescent light to the left. They had richer colors than under the daylight compact fluorescent to the right.

ANALYZE THE RESULTS

10. Sample answer: The LED bulb had the lowest wattage and the longest life but was also the most expensive. The halogen bulb was hottest and its light seemed whitest without being blue or yellow. The incandescent was the least expensive.

Connect TO THE ESSENTIAL QUESTION

11. Sample answers:

    For a hard-to-reach outdoor security light, you would want something with a long life so you wouldn't have to change it very often.

    For the hospital surgery room, you would want cool bright lights that make details stand out and help people keep alert.

    For reading lamps you would pick warm lights that are easy on the eyes and create a relaxed, comfortable feeling.

    For an artist's studio you would want bright bulbs that show colors the way they are supposed to look.

    For lighting a home in an area with high electric rates, you would want low wattage bulbs.

Answer Key for GUIDED Inquiry

DEVELOP A PLAN

3. a. Sample answer: We could look at the way the bulbs are made, their wattage, the color of their light, their lifetime, their cost, how bright they are, and whether they have any toxic materials in them.

b. Sample answer: We will set up half of the lamps on each side of the room and half on the other and look at the same things under each one. We will collect the information listed above for each lamp, and present the information in a data table.

ANALYZE THE RESULTS

5. Sample answer: The LED bulb had the lowest wattage and the longest life, but was also the most expensive. The halogen bulb was hottest and its light seemed whitest without being blue or yellow. The incandescent was the least expensive.

Connect TO THE ESSENTIAL QUESTION

6. Sample answers:

For a hard-to-reach outdoor security light, you would want something with a long life so you wouldn't have to change it very often.

For the hospital surgery room, you would want cool bright lights that make detail stand out and help keep people alert.

For reading lamps you would pick warm lights that are easy on the eyes and create a relaxed, comfortable feeling.

For the artist's studio you would want bright bulbs that show colors the way they are supposed to look.

For lighting a home in an area with high electric rates, you would want low wattage bulbs.

EXPLORATION LAB GUIDED *Inquiry*

Investigating Artificial Light

Homes, schools, and workplaces have commonly used incandescent and fluorescent tube bulbs to provide artificial light. New types of light bulbs are now also available to choose from. These include halogen lights, light-emitting diodes (LEDs), and several types of compact fluorescent bulbs. In this activity, you will examine some of these devices.

PROCEDURE

ASK A QUESTION

1 You will be using the results of this activity to explore the question: How are light bulbs different from one another?

RESEARCH A PROBLEM

2 Learn about the different kinds of light bulbs available as directed by your teacher.

MAKE OBSERVATIONS

3 Examine the bulbs and the light they provide at each station. Take notes about your observations on the lines provided. Things to do and notice are given in the following steps.

4 Look at how the bulb is made (without trying to take it apart). Describe it.

_____

_____

5 Use the thermometer to measure the air temperature near the bulb. Do not place the thermometer directly on the bulb.

_____

6 Describe the color temperature of the light. If a color graphic is available, estimate the color temperature in Kelvins. Otherwise, use color terms such as "yellow-white" or "bluish."

_____

_____

OBJECTIVE
• Compare the characteristics of several types of household light bulbs.

MATERIALS

For each station
• binders, empty (2)
• lamp
• light bulb, approx. 800 lumens
• light bulb color temperature graphic (optional)
• objects, small, colored (1 set)
• ruler, metric
• textbook
• thermometer

For each student
• safety goggles

Exploration Lab continued

7 Describe how the light seems to you, personally. For example, is it "warm," "friendly," "harsh," "crisp," or "bright"? Does it make you feel "alert," "calm," "anxious," or "welcomed?" Use your own words.

_____

_____

8 Note the wattage of the bulb below. To figure out how much energy a light bulb uses, you can multiply the wattage by the amount of time that the bulb is used.

_____

9 Compare the way objects look at each station with the way they look at other nearby stations. Do the colors look the same? Is the "feel" of the light the same? This is best done from about three meters away.

_____

_____

_____

ANALYZE THE RESULTS

10 **Making Generalizations** Review the information that you collected about the light bulbs. What patterns or generalizations can you make? Which bulbs had especially noticeable characteristics?

_____

_____

_____

Connect TO THE ESSENTIAL QUESTION

⓫ **Applying Concepts** You have looked at different technologies for producing artificial light. Choose three of the lighting situations below. Describe what you would consider when selecting an appropriate lighting technology for these situations.

• hard-to-reach outdoor security light
• task lighting for hospital surgery room
• work lights in an artist's studio
• lighting a home in an area with high electric rates
• reading lamps in a living room

_____

_____

_____

_____

_____

_____

ScienceFusion
Module J Lab Manual

142

Unit 3, Lesson 5
Light Technology

Original content Copyright © by Holt McDougal. Alterations to the original content are the responsibility of the instructor.

EXPLORATION LAB INDEPENDENT *Inquiry*

Investigating Artificial Light

Homes, schools, and workplaces have commonly used incandescent and fluorescent tube bulbs to provide artificial light. New types of light bulbs are now also available to choose from. These include halogen lights, light-emitting diodes (LEDs), and several types of compact fluorescent bulbs. In this activity, you will examine some of these devices.

PROCEDURE

ASK A QUESTION

1 You will be using the results of this activity to explore the question: How are light bulbs different from one another?

RESEARCH A PROBLEM

2 Learn about the different kinds of light bulbs available as directed by your teacher.

DEVELOP A PLAN

3 Look at the materials your teacher has provided for your study of artificial lighting.

a. Brainstorm with others to list observations you could make about the different kinds of lights so that you could compare them. List the observations here.

_____

_____

_____

_____

b. Work with others to plan how you are going to study the lights. What do you want to find out about the lights? Have your teacher approve the plan before you begin. Write your plan here.

_____

_____

_____

_____

OBJECTIVE

• Compare the characteristics of several types of household light bulbs.

MATERIALS

For each station

• binders, empty (2)
• lamp
• light bulb, approx. 800 lumens
• light bulb color temperature graphic (optional)
• objects, small, colored (1 set)
• ruler, metric
• textbook
• thermometer

For each student

• safety goggles

Exploration Lab continued

MAKE OBSERVATIONS

4 Follow your plan to observe the lights. Record your observations on a separate sheet of paper.

ANALYZE THE RESULTS

5 **Making Generalizations** Review the information that you collected about the light bulbs. What patterns or generalizations can you make? Which bulbs had especially noticeable characteristics?

_____

_____

_____

Connect TO THE ESSENTIAL QUESTION

6 **Applying Concepts** You have looked at different technologies for producing artificial light. Choose three of the lighting situations below. Describe what you would consider in selecting an appropriate lighting technology for these situations.

• hard-to-reach outdoor security light
• task lighting for hospital surgery room
• work lights in an artist's studio
• lighting a home in an area with high electric rates
• reading lamps in a living room

_____

_____

_____

_____

_____

_____